OVERVI

MOUNTAIN
BIKE

ORANGE
COUNTY

DAVID WOMACK

DISCLAIMER

This book is meant only as a guide to select trails within Orange County and does not guarantee rider safety in any way—have fun, but you ride at your own risk. Neither Menasha Ridge Press nor David Womack is liable for property loss or damage, personal injury, or death that result in any way from accessing or riding the trails described in the following pages. Be especially cautious when riding on or near boulders, steep inclines, and drop-offs, and do not attempt to explore terrain that may be beyond your abilities. To help ensure an uneventful ride, please read carefully the introduction to this book. Familiarize yourself thoroughly with the areas you intend to visit before venturing out. Ask questions and prepare for the unforeseen. Familiarize yourself with current weather reports, maps of the area you intend to visit, and any applicable trail regulations.

COPYRIGHT © 2008 BY DAVID WOMACK

All rights reserved
Published by Menasha Ridge Press
Printed in the United States of America
Distributed by Publishers Group West
First edition, first printing
Cover design by Travis Bryant
Text design by Steveco International
Cover photograph by David Womack
Author photograph by Mark O'Connor
Cartography and elevation profiles by David Womack and Chris Erichson

Library of Congress Cataloging-in-Publication Data
Womack, David, 1963–
Mountain bike! Orange County : a wide-grin ride guide / David Womack. — 1st ed.
p. cm.
ISBN-13: 978-0-89732-980-4
ISBN-10: 0-89732-980-5
1. Bicycle trails—California—Orange County—Guidebooks.
2. All terrain bicycles—California—Orange County—Guidebooks.
3. Orange County (Calif.)—Guidebooks. I. Title.
GV1045.5.C22O739 2008
388.1'20979496--dc22
2007026318

MENASHA RIDGE PRESS
P.O. BOX 43673
BIRMINGHAM, ALABAMA 35243
WWW.MENASHARIDGE.COM

CONTENTS

ACKNOWLEDGMENTS

First I'd like to thank Nathan Derge and GT Bicycles. It is impossible to write a mountain bike book without a bike. Moreover, there's something to be said for maximizing every moment in the saddle and riding every trail with confidence and satisfaction. GT kept me rolling, rubber side down, along the right path.

Thanks to all my riding partners, especially Mark O'Connor, Mark Garry, and Brandi Outwin, for being good sports, posing for photos, climbing just one more hill, and, for the most part, not complaining. Also, thanks to Curt Caprine for giving me a proper tour of The Fullerton Loop.

The maps in this book were rendered with a Garmin eTrex and TOPO! mapping software from National Geographic. Thanks to both of those companies for use of their fine products. The Garmin GPS proved to be a valuable tool—easy to use and trail worthy—and interfaced seamlessly with the TOPO! software.

Researching this book didn't merely involve riding the trails. Several park Web sites supplied valuable information, including the sites for Chino Hills, Crystal Cove, the Cleveland National Forest, and Orange County Regional Parks. GeoLadders.com provided great leads to new trails and ride times when I didn't trust my own. It's a great resource for all riders—I recommend joining.

Today, more Orange County trails than ever are open to mountain biking. The Warrior's Society and SHARE deserve special thanks for the maintenance of and advocacy for our local trails. Every local rider benefits from the work of these groups. Go to their Web sites if you are interested in volunteering your time.

Lastly, I'd like to thank Russell Helms and Menasha Ridge Press for showing confidence in me and giving me the opportunity to write this book. It's been a hoot.

NOTE ON THE SANTIAGO FIRE

Last week, just before this book went to press, a fire raged across eastern Orange County. An arsonist started the fire near Santiago Canyon Road. Blustery Santa Ana winds fueled the blaze as it raced across the region's rain-deprived canyons and hillsides. As of this writing, the fire has burned roughly 25,000 acres. This burn area includes nearly all of Whiting Ranch and the Irvine Ranch Land Reserve's Limestone Canyon. In the Cleveland National Forest the fire cut a swath across the Santa Ana Mountains from the Modjeska Grade to Live Oak Canyon Road and nearly all the way up to Main Divide Road. Parts of Silverado Canyon and Modjeska Canyon were also affected. Therefore, Santiago Truck Trail, The Luge, Harding Truck Trail, and Maple Springs Road all have been impacted by the fire. According to fire maps, the regions surrounding then Joplin Trail and The Silverado Motorway were not burned. However, the park is still closed and I have not witnessed any damage firsthand.

The good news is that fires play an essential role in Southern California's ecology. Trees will survive, plants will recover, and animals will find new homes. Some local plant species depend on fires to germinate their seeds. Springtime should beckon a miraculous recovery for the ash-covered hillsides. This does not justify careless behavior in the backcountry though. I have witnessed firsthand the devastation of Southern California wildfires. They are vicious, costly, and sometimes deadly. There is no excuse for starting any kind of fire in our local wilderness areas; always be careful and vigilant.

There will definitely be some trail closures in the fire-impacted areas. No official announcements have been made, so I can only estimate the length and breadth of these closures. Whiting Ranch suffered major damage and may be closed until trails can be repaired and, perhaps, until after the major rains of January and February. The Irvine Ranch Land Reserve, which manages Limestone Canyon, may hold off conducting docent-led rides in the region until spring of 2008. The Cleveland National Forest should be the first fire-affected area to open. The major dirt roads in the National Forest are vital thoroughfares, used daily by utility companies and geologists. The roads might be open to the public as soon as the fire is completely extinguished and the area is determined to be safe. However, if the park service deems that the fire risk is still too high, they could close the region to the public until we get some rain. If there isn't significant rainfall in the coming winter, the Cleveland National Forest could be subject to closures next summer and fall. It's too early too tell, so hopefully not. Check all of the park Web sites for current trail information and please respect all trail closures in the burn areas. Let nature take its course.

— *David Womack*
October 30, 2007

ABOUT THE AUTHOR

 David Womack is a California native and longtime Laguna Beach resident. As a child he spent his summers at El Morro Mobile Home Park but never ventured into El Morro Canyon. He has ventured there plenty as an adult—some might say too much.

David received his MFA in creative writing from UC Riverside in 2005. At Riverside he wrote plays and screenplays that have nothing to do with mountain biking. David is also an avid windsurfer, plays volleyball poorly, and enjoys a crossword or two.

PREFACE

I purchased my first mountain bike many years ago. I did so on the advice of a doctor. After three injuries in 18 months, he wanted me to give up basketball. He said, "You have the ankles of a racehorse," which apparently isn't good. So, short of resigning myself to the glue factory, I sought out a new sport.

Some of my friends had bikes, and I lived next door to Crystal Cove State Park, which was quickly becoming a very popular mountain bike destination. I bought what must have been the largest mountain bike ever made—a 24-inch Panasonic. My first efforts, along the user-friendly fire roads in Crystal Cove, were fairly incident free. Then, a friend (maybe I should say acquaintance) suggested I ride down Telonics, one of the steepest downhills in Laguna. So, I struggled up the long climb to Alta Laguna and looked for the trail. I found it, an unmitigated plummet into Laguna Canyon, and decided to go for it. I didn't even know to lower my bike seat, but if I had, it wouldn't have mattered. That Panasonic was huge. When the trail grew steep, it stopped functioning as a bicycle and transformed into a catapult. Unfortunately, I was the stone. By the time I reached the bottom of the hill, I had earned my merit badge for tumbling.

As with every sport, there is a learning curve for mountain biking. The initiation was even harsher before they made bikes that excelled at going downhill. My first years of trail riding were filled with difficulties, setbacks, and minor flesh wounds (if only the doctor had suggested croquet). However, there were also great experiences—riding with friends and exploring new places that were only a few miles from my home. I remember riding Laurel, Bommer, Willow, and Aliso and Wood canyons before the area was parceled up by development and riding from the El Morro Canyon to Turtle Rock without crossing a freeway.

Today the landscape of Orange County has changed somewhat, but there is still plenty of great riding. The bikes are better too. Over the course of writing this book, I've gained a new appreciation for the extent and diversity of Orange County's open space. Admittedly, some of the local parkland is crammed in between suburban development, but other recreational areas are vast and wild.

The 40 rides in this book are taken from several distinct areas in the county. I tried to cover as much of the region as possible—all the major riding areas are represented. I also tried to offer a variety of courses for riders of different intentions, expectations, and abilities. Some of the listed routes will challenge even the most accomplished riders, others will be appropriate for families, and still others will serve as useful training rides or after-work diversions.

Few of the local riding areas are contained within one municipality. Some border on several cities and communities. I have made a point to list multiple trailheads or access points for many of the mountain biking areas. Most Orange County residents should find at least a couple of rides within striking distance of their home. This is important, since life has its way of interfering with our conditioning and recreation schedule, and most people never have as much time as they need or want to ride.

Some rides, particularly those in the Cleveland National Forest, will involve more substantial driving and time commitments. These rides are not to be missed, though. If you are able to spend a day of your weekend climbing to the top of Saddleback or riding on the San Juan Trail, consider yourself fortunate. Not only will the experience be as good as any day of vacation, but you will burn enough calories to cover a full day of gluttony at a cruise-ship buffet.

Mountain biking may be many things to many riders—a means of conditioning, a source of adrenaline, or an escape from the doldrums of our everyday life—but it is always a release from the confines of pavement and concrete. You should view this book as an alternative map of Orange County. A map based on topographical features, not municipal boundaries. A map that takes you beyond the world of freeways, strip malls, and housing tracts into the world of canyons, ridgelines, and trails. This map probably won't reduce your driving time (although that would be greatly appreciated), but it should entice you to get out and ride.

And there are plenty of opportunities to ride—from the Chino Hills to San Mateo Canyon in San Clemente. Orange County has regional parks, state parks, city parks, a national forest, a major land reserve, and plenty of undesignated recreational areas. Nearly all of these areas have trails waiting to be accessed—great trails on varied terrain for riders of all skill levels. Some trails snake through cities and suburbs, maximizing every parcel of available open space. Other trails are so far removed from the suburban grid that, when you ride them, you won't believe you're in Orange County. One thing all the trails have in common is that they make use of land that was set aside. They exist within wilderness areas and parkland that will hopefully remain as such—for common use, for recreation, for escape, and for exploration. We all must value the open space we have left and vigilantly defend its worth.

Orange County is generally known for its freeways, strip malls, and theme parks. Disneyland's Matterhorn may be our most recognizable mountain. But before there was a South Coast Plaza and a Crystal Cathedral there were pristine coastal canyons, rolling hills, and, yes, mountain ranges. The 40 rides in this book access what remains of this less heralded, albeit magnificent, version of Orange County. Get out there and witness it for yourself. Ride the trails. You won't be disappointed.

— *David Womack*

RECOMMENDED RIDES

INTRODUCTION

What's Inside
The crux of this book is detailed information on 40 separate mountain bike rides. Some rides may have overlapping sections, but every ride contains distinct sections of trail and terrain. The chapters of the book represent major riding areas within the county. There may be several trailheads for each riding area and even some individual rides may have multiple trailhead options.

The Overview Map and Overview-map Key
Use the overview map on the inside front cover to find the location of each ride's primary trailhead. Each ride's number appears on the overview map, on the map key facing the overview map, in the table of contents, and at the top of the ride description's pages.

Trail Maps
Each ride contains a detailed map that shows the trailhead, the route, significant features, facilities, and topographic landmarks such as creeks, overlooks, and peaks. The author gathered map data by carrying a Garmin eTrex GPS unit while riding. GPS data was downloaded into a digital mapping program—*National Geographic* Topo!—and processed by expert cartographers to produce the highly accurate maps found in this book. Each trailhead's GPS coordinates are included with each profile (see below).

Elevation Profiles
Corresponding directly to the trail map, each ride contains a detailed elevation profile. The elevation profile provides a quick look at the trail from the side, enabling you to visualize how the trail rises and falls. Note the number of feet between each tick mark on the vertical axis (the height scale). To avoid making flat rides look steep and steep rides appear flat, appropriate height scales are used throughout the book to provide an accurate image of the ride's climbing difficulty. Elevation profiles for loop rides show total distance; those for out-and-back rides show only one-way distance.

GPS Trailhead Coordinates
In addition to GPS-based maps, this book also includes the GPS coordinates for each trailhead in two formats: latitude/longitude and UTM (Universal Transverse Mercator). Latitude/longitude coordinates employ a grid system that indicates your location by cross a line that runs north to south with a line that runs east to west. Lines of latitude are parallel and run in an east–west direction. The 0° line of latitude is the equator. Lines of longitude are not parallel, run in a north–south direction, and converge at the North and South poles. The 0° line of longitude passes through Greenwich, England.

Topographic maps show latitude and longitude as well as UTM grid lines. Known as UTM coordinates, the numbers index a specific point, also using a grid method. The survey information, or datum, used to arrive at the coordinates in this book is WGS84 (versus NAD27 or WGS83). For readers who own a GPS unit, whether handheld or onboard a vehicle, the latitude/longitude or UTM coordinates provided on the first page of each ride may be entered into the GPS unit. Just make sure your GPS unit is set to navigate using WGS84 datum. Now you can navigate directly to the trailhead.

Trailheads in parking areas can be reached by car, but some rides still require a short walk or ride to reach the official trailhead from the parking area. In those cases, a handheld unit is necessary to continue the GPS navigation process. That said, readers can easily access all trailheads in this book without a GPS unit by using the directions given, the overview map, and the trail map, which shows at least one significant road leading into the area. But for those who enjoy using the latest GPS technology to navigate, the necessary data have been provided. A brief explanation of the UTM coordinates for El Morro Canyon Loop (ride 20) follows.

UTM Zone 11S
Easting   0423594
Northing   3714293

The UTM zone number 11 refers to one of 60 vertical zones of the UTM projection, each of which is 6 degrees wide. The UTM zone letter S refers to horizontal zones, each of which is 8 degrees wide except for Zone X (12 degrees wide). The easting number 0423594 indicates in meters how far east or west a point is from the central meridian of the zone. Increasing easting coordinates on a topographic map or on your GPS screen indicate that you are moving east; decreasing easting coordinates indicate that you are moving west. The northing number 3714293 references in meters how far you are from the equator. Increasing northing coordinates indicate you are traveling north; decreasing northing coordinates indicate you are traveling south. To learn more about how to enhance your outdoor experiences with GPS technology, refer to *GPS Outdoors: A Practical Guide for Outdoor Enthusiasts* (Menasha Ridge Press).

Ride Description

Each ride description contains a detailed description of the route from beginning to end. The ride descriptions are the heart of this book. In each, the author provides a summary of the trail's essence and highlights any extras the ride has to offer. The route is clearly described, including landmarks, side trips, and possible alternate routes along the way. The main narrative is enhanced with an "In Brief" description of the ride, a Key at-a-Glance Information box, and driving directions to the trailhead. Many rides include an "After the Ride" note on nearby activities, such as where to grab a cold brew after the ride.

In Brief

A "taste of the ride." Think of this section as a snapshot focused on the historic landmarks, scenic vistas, and other sights you may encounter on the ride.

Scenic singletrack in Emerald Canyon

Key at-a-Glance Information

The information in the key at-a-glance box gives you quick statistics and specifics of each ride.

Length The length of the ride from start to finish (total distance traveled). There may be options to shorten or extend the ride, but the mileage corresponds to the ride as described. Consult the ride description for help deciding how to customize the ride for your ability or time constraints.

Configuration A description of the layout of the ride. Rides can be loops, out-and-backs, modified loops, and shuttle rides.

Aerobic Difficulty The physical effort needed to complete the ride. Rides are generally listed as easy, moderate, difficult, and very difficult. A brief explanation accompanies the rating.

Technical Difficulty The riding skill necessary to complete the ride. Rides are rated as easy, moderate, difficult, or extreme. A brief explanation details the nature of the trail's difficulties. Some rides, listed as "varied," may have options for riders of different skill levels. Some relatively difficult rides may be suitable for beginners if they are willing to dismount and walk sections that are beyond their abilities. Always ride within your limits and the limits of your bike. There is no shame in walking difficult terrain.

Exposure How much direct sunlight you can expect to encounter during the ride.

Scenery A short summary of what to expect in terms of plant life, wildlife, natural wonders, and scenic vistas.

Trail Traffic Indicates how busy the ride might be on an average day. Trail traffic, of course, varies from day to day and season to season. Weekend days typically see the most visitors.

Riding Time The range of time it takes to complete the ride. This time only includes time in the saddle and does not include time spent for rest, repairs, lunch, cell-phone conversations, and so on. Allow extra time for breaks (particularly on longer rides) and know your conditioning level and abilities.

Access Everything you need to get to the trailhead and legally ride the route: parking requirements, fees, permits, park regulations, and park hours.

Directions

Used in conjunction with the overview map, the driving directions lead you to the trailhead. Once at the trailhead, park only in designated areas.

After the Ride

An unbiased recommendation of where to eat or drink after riding in a particular area.

Weather

Weather in Orange County varies dramatically from region to region. In summer, inland temperatures may be as much as 30 degrees warmer than coastal temperatures. In winter, rain in Irvine may mean snow on Saddleback. Always be prepared for extremes. Canyons tend to run hotter during the day and cooler at night than open areas. Ridgelines and mountain peaks are subject to cold breezes. Temperatures at higher elevations may change abruptly.

Average Temperature by Month (Fahrenheit)

	January	February	March	April	May	June
High	68.1	69.4	70.2	72.7	74.5	77.8
Low	45.0	46.3	48.0	51.2	55.1	58.6

	July	August	September	October	November	December
High	82.7	84.1	83.6	79.3	73.7	68.8
Low	62.0	63.0	61.2	56.4	49.5	45.0

Expect hot (sometimes extremely hot) summertime temperatures in the inland areas of the county. Avoid midday rides in the Chino Hills, the Saddleback Valley, and Caspers Park during these months. The Chino Hills area also lies in the smog belt, so summertime heat generally worsens the air quality.

Coastal fog in the summer may cool the trails closer to the ocean. For this reason, Crystal Cove State Park is a popular summertime destination. Sometimes the fog burns off or doesn't extend very far inland. Be ready for swift temperature changes when riding inland from the coast.

Fall and winter bring the greatest variance between high and low temperatures. Warm afternoon rides may quickly turn into cold evening rides. Fall is also the time for the Santa Ana winds. These winds accelerate down the canyons, particularly those which are perpendicular with the shoreline (for example, El Morro and Emerald canyons). Santa Ana winds generally mean colder than average nights and may bring freezing temperatures to the Santa Ana Mountains (Cleveland National Forest).

January is historically the rainiest month in Southern California. However, in recent years, rainfall has tended to come later, and now March may be the rainiest month. January and February also tend to have several warm days—but again, be prepared for a quick temperature drop in the evening hours.

Weather in the spring is generally the least predictable. Storms tend to move quicker this time of year, fueled by stronger northwest winds. Never assume your April excursion into the Santa Ana Mountains will be warm and pleasant. Likewise, inland temperatures may soar to summertime levels. Always check the forecast before venturing out.

Water

Always err on the side of excess when deciding how much water to pack: a rider working hard in 90-degree heat needs about 10 quarts of fluid per day, or about 2.5 gallons. In other words, pack along one or two bottles even for short rides. For long rides, especially in hot weather, consider carrying water on your back in a hydration system.

With few exceptions, water is not available on the listed routes. Never drink water from the local streams—it's just not safe. Water fountains or faucets may be available along the ride, but don't depend on these. Plan ahead: bring enough water to accommodate your maximum time on the trail. Hydrate yourself before the ride and have water available for after the ride.

Clothing

For most areas of the county, shorts, gloves, a lightweight shirt, and a light Windbreaker will suffice. Winter excursions to higher elevations (such as the Santa Ana Mountains) may require additional layers and a warmer jacket. Full finger gloves are also recommended in the winter months. It's a good idea to wear long sleeves and leg protection on rides with narrow or overgrown trails. This will protect against ticks, poison oak, and scratches. Sunglasses will also protect you against eye injury on some of the tighter trails.

The Essentials

One of the first rules of riding is to be prepared for anything. The simplest way to be prepared is to carry the essentials. In addition to carrying the items listed on the next page, you need to know how to use them, especially the navigation items. Always consider worst-case scenarios, such as getting lost, riding back in the dark, broken components, cranking a wrist, or a brutal thunderstorm. The items in this list don't cost a lot of money, don't take up much room in a pack, and don't weigh much—but they just might save your life.

- **Compass** (and GPS unit if you have one)
- **Extra clothes:** rain protection, warm layers, gloves, warm hat
- **Extra food:** you should always have some left when you've finished riding
- **Fire:** windproof matches or lighter and fire starter
- **First-aid kit:** a compact, high-quality kit with instructions
- **Knife:** a bike multitool with a knife is best
- **Light:** flashlight or headlamp with extra bulbs and batteries
- **Map:** preferably a topo map and a copy of this book's trail map and ride description
- **Mirror:** to attract attention from aircraft in emergencies
- **Sun protection:** sunglasses, lip balm, sunblock, sun hat (in case you have to walk)
- **Water:** durable bottles and water treatment such as iodine or a filter

Topo Maps

The maps in this book have been produced with great care and, used with the directions, will direct you to the trail and help you stay on course. However, you will find additional detail and valuable information in the United States Geological Survey's 7.5-minute series topographic maps. Topo maps are available online and in many locations. The downside to USGS topo maps is that many of them are outdated, having been created 20 to 30 years ago. Cultural features on outdated topo maps, such as roads, will probably be inaccurate, but the topographic features should be accurate.

Digital topographic map programs such as Delorme's Topo USA enable you to review topo maps of the entire United States on your PC. Gathered while hiking with a GPS unit, you can also download GPS data onto the software and plot your own rides. Google Earth is a great free program that allows you to check aerial views of an area against a topo map.

If you're new to maps, you might be wondering what a topo map is. In short, a topo map indicates not only linear distance but elevation as well, using contour lines. Each brown squiggly line represents a particular elevation, and at the base of each topo, a contour's interval designation is given. If the contour interval is 20 feet, then the distance between each contour line is 20 feet. Follow five contour lines up on the same map, and the elevation has increased by 100 feet. Every fifth contour line is labeled with an altitude. These lines are slightly heavier than the intervening contour lines and are called the index lines. An index line that reads "1,300" indicates a contour that is 1,300 feet above sea level.

In addition to the outdoor shops listed in Appendix A, you'll find topo maps at major universities and some public libraries, where you can photocopy the maps you need (and avoid the cost of buying them). But if you want your own and can't find them locally, visit the United States Geological Survey Web site at **topomaps.usgs.gov.**

Also, don't overlook locally produced maps, which usually show superior detail for small areas. Examples include county road maps. Another reliable map source that contains

The Main Divide south of Santiago Peak

updated road information on topo maps is DeLorme's *Gazetteer* series. There is a *Gazetteer* for each of the 50 U.S. states.

Bike Tools

A few basic tools should be carried in a seat bag or in the pockets of your hydration pack. The most common problem is probably the dreaded flat. If you opt for carrying only compressed air to reinflate tires, you run the risk of having more flats than you have air cylinders. A small collapsible pump solves that problem. Before you go, make sure your tire-patch kit's rubber cement hasn't dried out. If your chain snaps, you'll need a chain tool to piece it back together. Below is a list of the essentials:

- Chain tool
- Duct tape
- Multitool
- Patch kit
- Spare tube
- Tire lever
- Tire pump and/or compressed-air kit

The multitool should address the balance of repairs or adjustments (seat, brakes, derailleurs) you may need to make on a ride. If you snap your frame in half, just call it a day and don't bother with the tools.

First-Aid Kit

A basic first-aid kit may contain more items than you might think necessary. Prepackaged kits in waterproof bags are available through Atwater Carey and Adventure Medical, to name two sources. Though there are quite a few items listed here, they pack into a small space:

- Ace bandages for sprains or to make compression bandages
- Antibiotic ointment (Neosporin or the generic equivalent) for cuts
- Aspirin, acetaminophen, ibuprofen, or naproxen for aches
- Band-Aids for cuts
- Benadryl or the generic equivalent diphenhydramine (in case of allergic reactions)
- Butterfly-closure bandages for deep cuts
- Epinephrine in a prefilled syringe (for people known to have severe allergic reactions to such things as bee stings)
- Gauze compress pads (a half dozen 4" x 4" pads) to clean and cover wounds
- Hydrogen peroxide or iodine for cuts, abrasions
- Insect repellent in case bugs are present
- Matches or pocket lighter to build fires for warmth, heating water, cooking food
- Roll of gauze to hold bandages on
- Sunscreen to prevent sunburn
- Whistle (it's more effective for signaling rescuers than your voice)

General Safety

Potentially dangerous situations can occur, but preparation and sound judgment usually result in safe forays into remote and wild areas. Here are a few tips to make your trip safer and easier.

Make sure your car, truck, or SUV is in good shape and check road conditions before you set out. If your vehicle breaks down, stay with it—it's easier to find a vehicle than a person.

Always carry food and water, whether you are planning an overnight trip or not. Food will give you energy, help keep you warm, and sustain you in an emergency situation until help arrives. Always bring water, or boil/filter/treat found water before drinking it.

- Wear sturdy biking shoes.
- Wear a professional-grade bike helmet (brain bucket).
- Never ride alone—take a buddy with you out on the trails.
- Tell someone where you're going and when you'll be back (be as specific as possible), and ask him or her to get help if you don't return in a reasonable amount of time.

Stay on the trails and routes described herein. Most riders who get lost do so when they leave the trail. Even on the most clearly marked trails, there is usually a point where you have to stop and consider which direction to head. If you become disoriented, don't panic. As soon as you think you may be lost, stop and assess your current direction, and then retrace your route back to the point where you went awry. Using a map, a compass, and this book, and keeping in mind what you have passed thus far, reorient yourself and trust your judgment on which way to continue. If you become absolutely unsure of how to proceed, return to your vehicle the way you came in. Should you become completely lost and have no idea of how to return to the trailhead, remaining in place along the trail and waiting for help is most often the best choice for adults and always the best option for kids. If you have prepared well, brought supplies, and taken that all-important step of telling someone where you'll be and for how long, staying in place shouldn't result in disaster.

Take along your brain. A cool, calculating mind is the single most important piece of equipment you'll need on the trail. Think before you act. Watch your step. Plan ahead. Avoiding accidents before they happen is the best recipe for a rewarding and relaxing ride.

Ask questions. It's a lot easier to get advice beforehand and avoid mishaps away from civilization, where finding help may be difficult. Use your head when venturing out into the backcountry.

Ticks

Ticks are commonly found in brushy and woody areas. Ticks, which are arthropods and not insects, need a host to feast on in order to reproduce. The ticks that light on you while you are riding will be very small, sometimes so tiny that you won't be able to spot them. Primarily of two varieties, deer ticks and dog ticks, they need a few hours of actual attachment before they can transmit any disease they may harbor. Ticks may settle in shoes, socks, or hats. The best strategy is to visually check every so often while riding; do a thorough check before you get in the car; and then, when you take a postride shower, do an even more thorough check of your entire body. Ticks that haven't attached are easily removed but not easily killed. If you pick off a tick while on the trail, just toss it aside. If you find one on your body at home, remove it and then send it down the toilet. For ticks that have embedded, removal with tweezers is best.

Snakes

Rattlesnakes are the only dangerous snakes in Orange County. However, for the most part, you either have to be very careless or very unlucky to be bitten by one. Rattlesnakes do not viciously attack people, they merely fight back when cornered or frightened. Leave them alone. When you encounter a rattlesnake on the trail (if you don't see it, you will generally hear the rattle) give it a respectfully wide berth. The snakes can strike about half the distant of their bodies, but may look smaller when coiled. As a rule, avoid prompting snakes to coil. In the rare case of a rattlesnake bite, remain calm and call for help if it is available—otherwise take the easiest route back to the trailhead and go immediately to a hospital for treatment.

Mountain Lions

Many of the local riding areas have warning signs for mountain lions. There is a reason for this: there have been three local attacks in the last 20 years, including two involving mountain bikers. However, encounters with mountain lions are extremely rare, and your chances of being attacked are next to miniscule. But that doesn't mean you shouldn't be vigilant. Here are a few helpful guidelines for mountain lion encounters:

- Keep kids close to you. Observed in captivity, mountain lions seem especially drawn to small children.
- Try to make yourself look larger by raising your arms and/or opening your jacket if you're wearing one
- Do not run from a mountain lion. Running may stimulate the animal's instinct to chase.
- Do not approach a mountain lion. Instead, give it room to get away.
- Do not crouch or kneel down. These movements could make you look smaller and more like the lion's prey.
- Try to convince the lion you are dangerous—not its prey. Without crouching, gather nearby stones or branches and toss them at the animal. Slowly wave your arms above your head and speak in a firm voice.

If all fails and you are attacked, fight back. People have successfully fought off an attacking lion with rocks and sticks. Try to remain facing the animal, and fend off attempts to bite at your head or neck—a lion's typical aim.

Poison Oak

Poison oak is primarily recognized by its three-leaflet configuration—on either a vine or shrub. Usually within 12 to 14 hours of exposure (but sometimes much later), raised lines and/or blisters will appear, accompanied by a terrible itch. Urushiol, the oil in the sap of this plant, is responsible for the rash. Refrain from scratching, since bacteria under fingernails can cause infection; you can also spread the rash to other parts of your body by scratching. Wash and dry the rash thoroughly, applying a calamine lotion or other product to help dry the rash. If itching or blistering is severe, seek medical attention. Remember that oil-contaminated clothes, pets, or riding gear can easily cause an irritating rash on you or someone else, so be sure to wash exposed parts of your body, exposed clothes, gear, and pets.

Trail Etiquette

- When riding through local open space always remember that great care and resources (from nature as well as from your tax dollars) have gone into creating these trails. Treat the trail, wildlife, and fellow riders with respect.

- Ride on open trails only. Respect trail and road closures (ask if not sure), avoid trespassing on private land, obtain permits and authorization as required, and leave gates as you found them or as marked.
- Leave only tire prints. Pack out what you pack in. No one likes to see the trash someone else has left behind.
- Never intentionally spook animals. An unannounced approach, a sudden movement, or a loud noise startles most animals. A surprised animal can be dangerous to you, to others, and to the animal itself.
- Plan ahead. Know your bike, your ability, and the area in which you are riding—and prepare accordingly. Be self-sufficient at all times; carry necessary supplies for changes in weather or other conditions.
- Be courteous to other riders, equestrians, and all others you encounter on the trails; maintaining a wide grin makes this task a lot easier.

CHINO HILLS

01

NORTH RIDGE LOOP (GILMAN PEAK)

KEY AT-A-GLANCE INFORMATION

Length: 10.2 miles
Configuration: Loop with 0.8-mile out-and-back (0.4 miles each way)
Aerobic difficulty: Moderate; 4 miles of climbing hurts less than you'd think.
Technical difficulty: Easy to moderate; the downhill on Sycamore Trail is fast and fun. Telegraph Canyon has a few easy stream crossings.
Exposure: Mostly complete sun
Scenery: Great views of eastern Orange County from the ridgeline; Telegraph Canyon follows a creek.
Trail traffic: Light on the ridge; moderate in the canyon
Riding time: 1–1.5 hours
Access: The ride begins and ends at the Carbon Canyon entrance to Chino Hills State Park. Parking at Carbon Canyon Regional Park is $3 weekdays and $5 weekends. When an attendant is not present, you will need somewhat crisp dollar bills for the parking kiosk. Open Nov. 1–Mar. 31, 7 a.m.–6 p.m.; Apr. 1–Oct. 31, 7 a.m.–9 p.m.
Special comments: The best months to ride the Chino Hills are Nov.–Apr. Daytime temperatures soar in summer months, as does the air-pollution index.

GPS TRAILHEAD COORDINATES (WGS 84)

UTM Zone (WGS84) 11S
Easting   0423332
Northing 3753727
Latitude N 33°55'16"
Longitude W 117°49'46"

In Brief

Carbon Canyon Regional Park is the primary access point to the western end of Chino Hills State Park. This ride begins at the base of Telegraph Canyon and then quickly turns to ascend the North Ridge Road. A long, gradual push up the ridge road tops out at Gilman Peak. The route continues another mile past the peak to the Sycamore Trail. The drop down the Sycamore Trail bottoms out at Telegraph Canyon. The last 4-plus miles are almost completely downhill, cranking through the narrow canyon to complete the loop.

Information

Carbon Canyon Regional Park
4442 Carbon Canyon Road
Brea, CA 92823
(714) 973-3160

Description

The Telegraph Canyon trailhead is across from the interpretive center at Carbon Canyon Regional Park. The trail, a dirt road, initially parallels Carbon Canyon Road, but then cuts away from the road toward Telegraph Canyon. The dirt road runs through a bit of open terrain near the confluence of Telegraph and Carbon canyons. This area is apparently a flood plain for nearby Carbon Canyon Dam.

At 0.4 miles two paths split left, away from Telegraph Canyon Road. The first is a singletrack along Carbon

DIRECTIONS

From the CA 5 and CA 55 freeway interchange: Take CA5 north 4.1 miles to CA 57. Follow CA 57 north 10.1 miles and exit at Lambert Road (Exit 10). Turn right and follow East Lambert Road 1.8 miles to the stoplight at Carbon Canyon Road. Continue straight on Carbon Canyon Road for 0.4 miles, then turn right into Carbon Canyon Regional Park. After you pay at the entrance, turn left. The trailhead is at the east end of the parking lot.

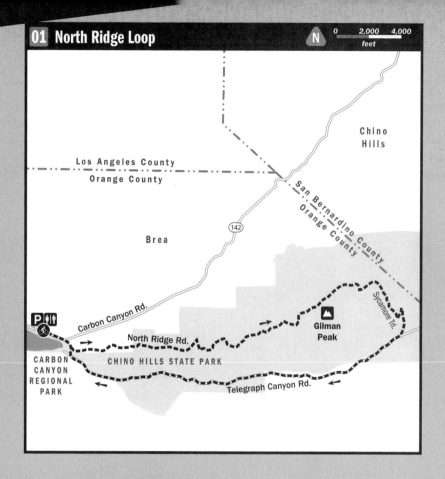

N

0   2,000   4,000
feet

Chino Hills

Los Angeles County
Orange County

San Bernardino County
Orange County

Brea

142

Carbon Canyon Rd.

North Ridge Rd.

Gilman Peak

Sycamore Trl.

CARBON CANYON REGIONAL PARK

CHINO HILLS STATE PARK

Telegraph Canyon Rd.

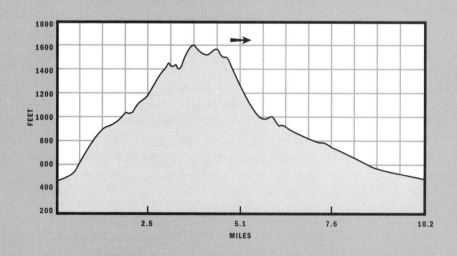

FEET

1800
1600
1400
1200
1000
800
600
400
200

2.5   5.1   7.6   10.2
MILES

The trailhead at Carbon Canyon Regional Park

Canyon. Although this trail looks tempting, it's fairly sandy, following a short course along the Carbon Canyon riverbed, and seems more appropriate for equestrians than bikes. Take the second left and begin the ascent of the North Ridge. North Ridge Road is sometimes referred to as the Four Mile Climb, however most of the climbing is completed in merely 3 miles. Even 3 miles of climbing may still sound daunting to some, but it shouldn't—it's a gradual climb on a smooth, hard-packed fire road. The steepest part is at the beginning, and even that's not so bad. Good climbers will be able to make most of the climb in the middle chainring. Moderate climbers will necessarily alternate between the granny gear and the middle chainring.

As you climb the ridge, you'll be afforded views of Carbon Canyon, Telegraph Canyon, and, on clear winter days, much of the Orange County basin. After 3 miles the climb tops out and then follows the undulating ridgeline before making the final push around Gilman Peak. A fire road that reaches the peak itself veers right from the North Ridge Trail at 3.9 miles. There is a lookout tower atop the peak, which rises only about 50 feet above North Ridge Road. From just below the peak, a singletrack cuts down to Telegraph Canyon. Unfortunately, state park officials closed this trail to mountain bikes a few years ago.

The legal drop to Telegraph Canyon is on the Sycamore Trail. Roll along the North Ridge to 4.8 miles and look for a small sign designating the trail. The Sycamore Trail begins as a doubletrack—it's a fast, nontechnical downhill with some fun turns and few, if any, surprises. Past a couple of wide-open switchbacks, the trail runs straight and then narrows to a singletrack. The singletrack follows a narrow canyon and then cuts across a small streambed to join Telegraph Canyon Road at 5.9 miles.

The top of the Sycamore Trail

Veer right on Telegraph Canyon Road. After a very brief climb, the trail runs slightly downhill almost all the way back to the trailhead. Crank hard—it's a fun ride. The dirt road carves through the narrow canyon, dipping and winding through plenty of turns. Signs along the canyon limit speed to 15 mph. Take heed and, as always, be respectful of hikers and other trail users. Luckily most of the turns along the canyon have good lines of visibility.

The canyon has several mature sycamore and oak trees fed by the year-round creek. The creek also crosses Telegraph Canyon Road at a few points. None of these crossings are technically daunting, but they can be muddy. Generally, there are planks or stepping stones to appease the dirt averse.

At 8.5 miles you'll pass the cutoff to the Diemer Trail, named for the large water filtration plant that lies atop the South Ridge. Continue down Telegraph Canyon Road toward the base of Telegraph Canyon. At 10 miles you'll pass the North Ridge Road to complete the loop. Retrace the last 0.4 miles to the trailhead.

After the Ride

Look for the Durango Mexican Grill on Imperial Highway, just west of CA 57 near downtown Brea. It's an unpretentious deli-style Mexican café. There's plenty of variety to please most palates and a better-than-average salsa bar for some postride spice.

Durango Mexican Grill
730 East Imperial Highway
Brea, CA 92821
(714) 255-5663

02

RAPTOR RIDGE RIDE

KEY AT-A-GLANCE
INFORMATION

Length: 17.6 miles
Configuration: 13.6-mile out-and-back with 4-mile loop
Aerobic difficulty: Moderate; the ride is lengthy but not difficult.
Technical difficulty: Easy to moderate; the singletrack is more scenic than adrenaline inducing.
Exposure: Mostly complete sun
Scenery: Lush canyon foliage, wide-open grassy hillsides, and views of the San Gabriel and San Bernardino mountain ranges
Trail traffic: Telegraph Canyon gets busy, particularly near the Carbon Canyon entrance and close to the Four Corners area.
Riding time: 1.5–2.5 hours
Access: The ride begins and ends at the Carbon Canyon entrance to Chino Hills State Park. Parking at Carbon Canyon Regional Park runs $3 weekdays and $5 weekends. When an attendant is not present, you will need somewhat crisp dollar bills for the parking kiosk. Open Nov. 1–Mar. 31, 7 a.m.–6 p.m.; Apr. 1–Oct. 31, 7 a.m.–9 p.m.

In Brief

Start at Carbon Canyon Regional Park and crank 6 miles up Telegraph Canyon. The Raptor Ridge Trail begins at Four Corners. Follow the singletrack, winding through the grassy hillsides all the way to Upper Aliso Canyon Road. A short downhill leads to the Rolling M Ranch (the terminus of Bane Canyon Road). The eastern end of Telegraph Canyon Road begins just past the ranch. Head back on Telegraph Canyon Road for a bit, and then climb a utility road back to the Raptor Ridge Trail. After a short climb, it's all downhill. Cruise down the singletrack to Four Corners and then rip down Telegraph Canyon, quickly retracing the first 6 miles of the ride, to the trailhead.

Information

Carbon Canyon Regional Park
4442 Carbon Canyon Road
Brea, CA 92823
(714) 973-3160

Description

Telegraph Canyon Road runs well beyond the geographical boundary of Telegraph Canyon, climbing past Four Corners and running all the way east to Bane Canyon. This particular route covers that distance, utilizing much of Telegraph Canyon Road. However, past Four Corners,

GPS TRAILHEAD
COORDINATES (WGS 84)
UTM Zone (WGS84) 11S
Easting 0423333
Northing 3753727
Latitude N 33°55'16"
Longitude W 117°49'46"

DIRECTIONS

From the CA 5 and CA 55 interchange: Take CA 5 north 4.1 miles to CA 57. Follow CA 57 north 10.1 miles and exit at Lambert Road (Exit 10). Turn right and follow East Lambert Road 1.8 miles to the stoplight at Carbon Canyon Road. Continue straight on Carbon Canyon Road for 0.4 miles, then turn right into Carbon Canyon Regional Park. After you pay at the entrance, turn left. The trailhead is at the east end of the parking lot.

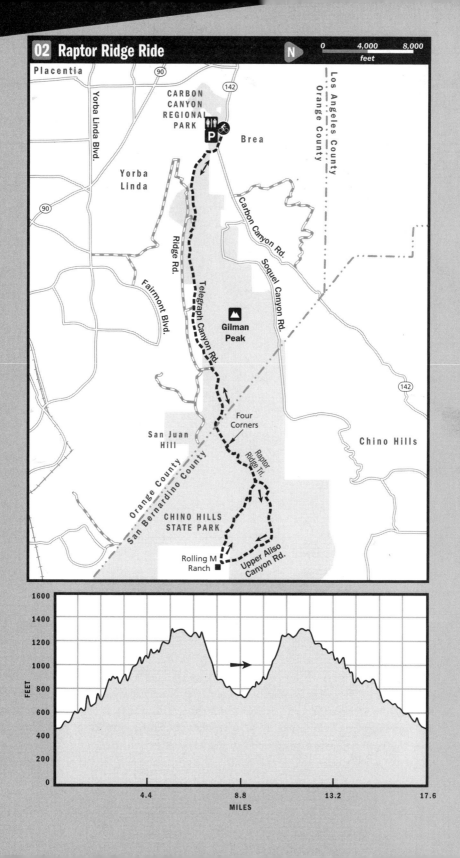

N

0   4,000   8,000
feet

Placentia

90

Yorba Linda Blvd.

CARBON CANYON REGIONAL PARK

142

Brea

Los Angeles County
Orange County

Yorba Linda

90

Ridge Rd.

Fairmont Blvd.

Carbon Canyon Rd.

Soquel Canyon Rd.

Telegraph Canyon Rd.

Gilman Peak

142

Four Corners

San Juan Hill

Raptor Ridge Trl.

Chino Hills

Orange County
San Bernardino County

CHINO HILLS STATE PARK

Rolling M Ranch

Upper Aliso Canyon Rd.

1600
1400
1200
1000
800
600
400
200
0

FEET

4.4   8.8   13.2   17.6

MILES

Telegraph Canyon Road heading up toward San Juan Hill

you'll take a satisfying diversion on the Raptor Ridge Trail—allowing for some fun and scenic singletrack riding while avoiding some unnecessary and unrewarded climbing on the canyon road.

You'll find the Telegraph Canyon trailhead across from the nature trail at Carbon Canyon Regional Park. The trail initially follows the fence line adjacent to Carbon Canyon Road. Just past a gate the trail widens to a dirt road and veers away from Carbon Canyon. Stay right at the turnoff to the North Ridge Trail, following the road as it winds eastward into the mouth of Telegraph Canyon.

The ride up the canyon can be managed in middle to large gears. Really. There is roughly only 800 feet of elevation gain in 6 miles. The road is mostly smooth and hard packed, the only obstacles being a few fun and easy stream crossings.

Past the intersection with Little Canyon Road, the canyon narrows and the road winds above the adjacent creek bed. Collections of oaks, sycamores, and willows provide a nice respite from the sun. Push through the turns but be mindful of other cyclists charging downhill. The canyon widens at Four Corners—a crossroads for several trails and the geographic center of Chino Hills State Park. If you need a break, there is a shaded rest area with a picnic table and bike racks.

At 6 miles veer left from Four Corners and head up the Raptor Ridge Trail. The singletrack climbs initially, then courses along a grassy hillside. At 6.6 miles the trail joins a utility road. Stay left and rejoin the trail just past the utility pole. Take in the picturesque views of the San Gabriel Mountains as you follow the singletrack downhill to Upper Aliso Canyon. The drop is neither steep nor technical but can be a little bumpy due to equestrian use.

Near 7.8 miles the grasslands give way to Upper Aliso Canyon. Turn right on Upper Aliso Canyon Road and follow the gentle grade down to the Rolling M Ranch. Follow paved Bane Canyon Road past the ranch and the parking lot. At 9 miles, just beyond the turnoff to the parking lot, turn right and head through a gate to Telegraph Canyon Road. Push up the road, heading westward. At 9.9 miles turn right and head up the utility road. This is the steepest and longest climb of the ride, but it is worth it to avoid the even longer (and unrewarding) climbs up Telegraph Canyon. The climb switchbacks and passes through an intersection with another road. Stay left and climb to the highest utility tower. Near 10.9 miles you will rejoin the first section of the Raptor Ridge Trail. The singletrack descends easily to Four Corners.

If you feel up to another climb, take the Bovine's Delight Trail to the South Ridge or the Sycamore Canyon Trail up to the North Ridge. Both of these ridges parallel Telegraph Canyon. Foregoing another climb, crank back down Telegraph Canyon Road. The ride home is fun and fast. Wind out through the trees near the top and then push all the way through the rest of the canyon. You'll make a good splash as you power through the stream crossings close to the end of the ride. The last mile or so offers a generous amount of time to cool down. Perhaps you can take the time to contemplate your next ride.

Note: The best months to ride in Chino Hills are October through May. Excessive heat and air pollution make for undesirable riding conditions during the summer months. The eastern part of this ride may be accessed from Bane Canyon Road in Chino Hills. It is also possible to do a slightly modified version of the ride beginning at the park's Rimcrest entrance in Yorba Linda.

After the Ride

Follow Carbon Canyon and East Lambert roads back toward CA 57. Just before the overpass, turn right on Pointe Drive and head up to the Soup Plantation. Yes, it's all you can eat, ostensibly healthy, inexpensive, and casual enough to allow showing up with a bit of postride grit. OK, it's not great cuisine, but if you rode hard, the food will certainly taste good.

Soup Plantation
555 Pointe Drive, Building #2
Brea, CA 92821-3672
(714) 990-4773

03

KEY AT-A-GLANCE INFORMATION

KEY AT-A-GLANCE INFORMATION

Length: 6.9 miles

Configuration: Loop with 1.8-mile out-and-back (0.9 miles each way)

Aerobic difficulty: The ride is short, but there are plenty of steep intervals to get your heart pumping.

Technical difficulty: Easy; the entire route is butter smooth.

Exposure: Almost entirely complete sun

Scenery: Great views from the South Ridge to Saddleback, Mount Baldy, and the entire Orange County Basin. On clear days, you can see Catalina Island.

Trail traffic: Light to moderate; the greatest concentration of park users is in Telegraph Canyon.

Riding time: 45 minutes–1.25 hours

Access: Free parking is available on Rimcrest Drive near the trailhead. Be respectful of the local residents when arriving and leaving. The entire ride takes place in Chino Hills State Park.

Special comments: There are no facilities at this park entrance. However, a kiosk at the trailhead dispenses park maps.

GPS TRAILHEAD COORDINATES (WGS 84)

UTM Zone (WGS84) 11S
Easting 0427880
Northing 3752347
Latitude N 33°54'33"
Longitude W 117°46'48"

SOUTH RIDGE AND TELEGRAPH CANYON LOOP

In Brief

Enter the state park at Rimcrest Drive and start climbing. The South Ridge Trail ascends to San Juan Hill in a series of steep intervals. Forego the final climb to the peak and turn left on the Bovine's Delight Trail. The singletrack parallels the ridge for nearly 0.5 miles and then makes a smooth and gradual drop to Four Corners. Turn left on Telegraph Canyon Road—the narrow canyon is both scenic and fun to ride. Whip through the tight turns, heading downhill for a couple miles to the Little Canyon Trail. A steep but forgivably short climb up Little Canyon leads back to the South Ridge. Retrace the ridge, rolling primarily downhill, to conclude the ride.

Information

Chino Hills State Park
1879 Jackson Street
Riverside, CA 92504
(909) 780-6222
Note: the above address is nowhere near the trailhead

Description

Rimcrest Drive is a convenient access point to Chino Hills State Park, particularly for residents of Eastern Orange County. Via the CA 241 tollway, it is also the closest Chino

DIRECTIONS

From CA 5 and CA 55 freeway interchange: Take CA 55 north 8 miles and merge onto CA 91 east. Go 2.1 miles on CA 91 and exit at Imperial Highway (CA 90). Turn left, follow Imperial Highway 1.5 miles, and then exit at Kellogg Drive. Turn right on Kellogg Drive, go 1.1 miles, and then turn right on Yorba Linda Boulevard. Continue 0.2 miles and turn left onto Fairmont Boulevard. Follow Fairmont Boulevard 1.6 miles to Rimcrest Drive. Turn left and follow Rimcrest Drive uphill 0.3 miles and park. The trailhead is just before where the road curves left and becomes Blue Gum Drive.

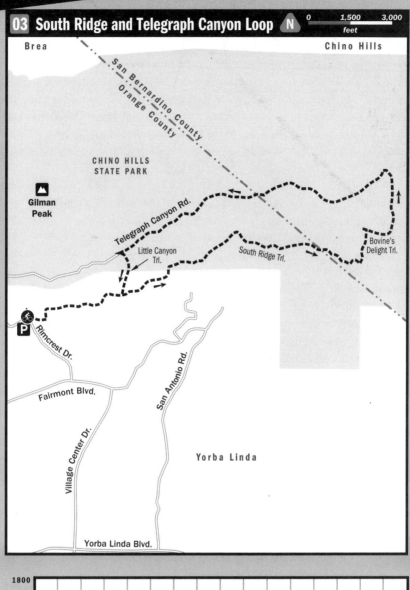

N

| 0 | 1,500 | 3,000 |
feet

Brea   Chino Hills

San Bernardino County
Orange County

CHINO HILLS
STATE PARK

Gilman
Peak

Telegraph Canyon Rd.

Little Canyon
Trl.

South Ridge Trl.

Bovine's
Delight Trl.

P

Rimcrest Dr.

Fairmont Blvd.

San Antonio Rd.

Village Center Dr.

Yorba Linda

Yorba Linda Blvd.

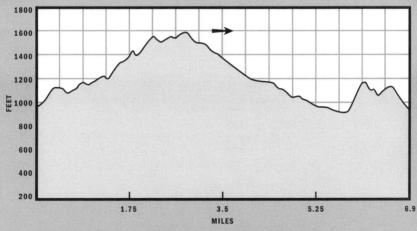

FEET

1800
1600
1400
1200
1000
800
600
400
200

1.75   3.5   5.25   6.9

MILES

Hills access point for South Orange County residents (if those riders don't mind passing up prime riding spots in the Santa Ana Mountains to get there).

What Chino Hills State Park lacks in technical singletracks it makes up for with spaciousness. You can cover a lot of miles in this park without riding the same trail twice. This particular loop is relatively short, but it could be made longer by adding a loop around Raptor Ridge or an additional climb to the North Ridge from Four Corners. As is, the nearly 7-mile loop is a great training ride—a perfect after-work jaunt with plenty of steep climbing intervals. Good climbers will easily finish the loop in an hour or less.

Where Rimcrest Drive bends into Blue Gum Drive, look for a dirt road running to the right of the corner house. After 50 yards, you will pass through a gate to the South Ridge Trail. There is an information kiosk with useful maps, directly across from gate. This is also the trailhead for the Easy Street Trail, but unfortunately it is closed to bicycles.

Head east on South Ridge Trail and begin climbing immediately. The grade is pretty steep, but the dirt is hard packed and rut free, allowing for efficient climbing. Within 0.3 miles you will be well above the nearby rooftops. The road continues to gain altitude, following the undulating ridge, dropping gradually, and then climbing in short, steep intervals.

The cutoff to Little Canyon comes at 0.9 miles. Stay on the ridge. The late afternoon and evening views are particularly stunning. Just after sunset, the entire Orange County basin will be dotted with lights. Look for distant Catalina Island on clear days.

Keep climbing till nearly 2.5 miles. You'll see the Bovine's Delight Trail on the left well before the road reaches the top of San Juan Hill. Veer left on the singletrack and follow it as it twists along just below the ridgeline. There aren't any bovines, but the trail is fun and scenic. The narrow path, hard packed and smooth, cuts between tall grass and trees. Near 3 miles a dead-end trail cuts off to the left, but you stay right, heading gradually downhill. The last section of trail runs straight out of a narrow canyon and ends at Four Corners.

Four Corners marks the confluence of Telegraph Canyon Road, Raptor Ridge Road, Bovine's Delight, and the utility road to the North Ridge. Four Corners is to Chino Hills State Park what Kansas is to the United States—the middle of everything. Foregoing a longer ride, head left (west) on the Telegraph Canyon Trail. The next 2 miles run fast and easy, winding down the tree-lined canyon. You'll have plenty of time to regain your stamina before the last climb.

Just before you reach 5.8 miles, look for the Little Canyon Trail. The dirt road climbs straight up to the South Ridge. It's a steep climb, but it doesn't last long. The traction is good, so there's no excuse not to stand up in the saddle and grind through the last steep section. You can push yourself hard, knowing the ride is almost over.

Turn right on the South Ridge Trail at 6.1 miles. There is only one small climb left, so you can enjoy the view as you warm down. The last 0.4 miles run straight downhill to your parking spot.

Note: Fall, winter, and spring are the best times to ride in Chino Hills State Park. Daytime temperatures may reach three digits during the summer months, and the smog is no picnic either.

04

KEY AT-A-GLANCE INFORMATION

Length: 8.4 miles

Configuration: Loop with 1-mile out-and-back (0.5 miles each way)

Aerobic difficulty: Short; strenuous

Technical difficulty: Moderate; generous amount of fun and scenic singletrack, but no difficult downhilling; a few technical climbs.

Exposure: Mostly complete sun

Scenery: Grass-covered hills with tree-lined arroyos; stunning views of Mount Baldy and the San Bernardino Mountains; cows

Trail traffic: Moderate to heavy on Bane Canyon (including cars); light on the singletracks

Riding time: 1.25–2 hours

Access: Free parking on Sapphire Street near the Bane Canyon entrance to Chino Hills State Park. Open Nov. 1–Mar. 31, 7 a.m.–6 p.m.; Apr. 1–Oct. 31, 7 a.m.–9 p.m.

Special comments: Bane Canyon Road is generally open to traffic. Cars may use this drive to access the center of the park. It is possible to do this loop from the interior parking area near the Rolling M Ranch, but the preferable starting point is at the base of Bane Canyon Road.

GPS TRAILHEAD COORDINATES (WGS 84)

UTM Zone (WGS84) 11S
Easting 0435097
Northing 3757346
Latitude N 33°57'17"
Longitude W 117°42'09"

In Brief

This loop utilizes some of the least-used trails in Chino Hills State Park. Begin at the Bane Canyon entrance and climb into the state park. Before you get to the entrance gate, turn right on the Bane Ridge Trail and continue climbing. From the top of the ridge, veer right and head down the Sidewinder Trail. The singletrack wraps around a grassy hillside and then courses along a creek bed to the Upper Aliso Canyon Trail. Head left on this trail, cruise downhill to the Rolling M Ranch, and pick up Bane Canyon Road. After a short ride on the pavement, climb up the McClean Overlook Road to the East Fenceline Trail. This singletrack runs along the eastern boundary of the park, following a remote path, dipping and winding through grassland and shady arroyos. A final steep climb leads back to Bane Canyon Road, and then a short shot downhill leads back to the trailhead.

Information

Chino Hills State Park
1879 Jackson Street
Riverside, CA 92504
(909) 780-6222
Note: the above address is nowhere near the trailhead.

Description

Turn right off Sapphire Road and then push up Bane Canyon Road—the climb is steepest at the start but eases

DIRECTIONS

From the intersection of CA 5 and CA 55 freeways: Take CA 55 freeway north 8 miles and merge onto CA 91 freeway east. Go 11.9 miles and exit onto CA 71 (Corona Expressway) north. Follow CA 71 6.8 miles and exit at Soquel Canyon Parkway. Turn left on Soquel Canyon Parkway and continue 1.1 miles to Elinvar Drive. Turn left on Elinvar Drive and head uphill. The trailhead is just past where Elinvar Drive becomes Sapphire Road.

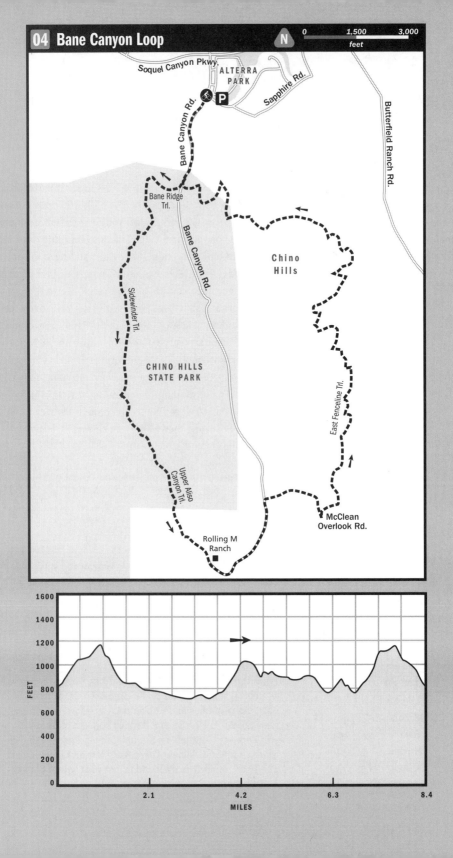

somewhat around the first turn. The road, a mix of dirt and gravel, is open to vehicles. The incessant washboard should limit traffic speeds, but keep your eyes open. After 0.5 miles the road levels into Bane Canyon. The main park entrance is straight ahead, but, unless you need a park map, veer right. Proceed through a gate and crank up the Bane Ridge Trail. The dirt road climbs another 0.5 miles to a utility tower.

At 1 mile, instead of continuing straight on the Bane Ridge Trail, now a singletrack, turn right and head down a utility road. Before you get to the utility tower, veer right onto the Sidewinder Trail. The singletrack courses around a grassy hillside and then drops gently down to a creek bed. Near 1.4 miles keep left (don't climb straight) and follow the Sidewinder Trail. Dart down a grassy trail, coursing in and out of the tree-lined creek bed. This is a great trail, but it suffers from lack of use and proximity to the waterway. Particularly in spring, the grass and foliage may encroach upon the trail. Keep an eye out for downed branches and other obstructions. You may have to portage your bike a bit if sections of the trail are washed out or blocked.

After 2 miles the Sidewinder Trail runs into the Upper Aliso Canyon Trail, a dirt road. Turn left and cruise down the road to the Rolling M Ranch. Continue straight past the ranch on a paved section of Bane Canyon Road. Yes, paved. This interior section of Bane Canyon is the only paved section of the road: such are the mysteries of the California State Parks.

At 3.8 miles turn right and head up McClean Overlook Road. Stay right, avoiding the left fork into an unnamed canyon, and climb. Before you reach the overlook, at 4.1 miles, cut left on the East Fenceline Trail. Follow the trail back toward the ridgeline. The first section of the trail is somewhat damaged from equestrian use and a bit bothersome to ride. If you are nonplussed at this point, don't worry—it gets better. Soon the trail crosses the ridge and drops down to the eastern edge of the state park, cutting a path just above a series of cow pastures. Wind along the hillside path, dropping into tight arroyos and then climbing around hillside knolls. Push into the turns, but stay in a low gear since some of the short climbs are steep and taxing.

At 5.6 miles an unnamed dirt road veers left. Stay right and on the trail, enjoying a hopefully clear view of the San Gabriel Mountains to the northeast. Near 6 miles the trail drops steeply into a tight, tree-filled canyon. The climb out of the canyon is short but steeply uphill. By this time, you'll realize this narrow singletrack keeps going and, almost improbably, going. A second downhill leads to what seems to be an even more-remote trail section. The path traverses a sharp hillside running through a thicket of trees. This section tends to be a bit overgrown. There may be obstructions on the trail, but they should be easy to get through: just keep forging ahead. The final climb begins near 6.7 miles; it's a brutish grade, rising near 400 feet in just over half a mile. Give it your all, since the rest of the ride is gravy.

At 7.4 miles the singletrack ends at a dirt road. Turn left and head down to Bane Canyon Road. At 7.8 miles turn right and retrace the first part of the ride. The final cruise is all downhill.

05

SCULLY RIDGE LOOP

KEY AT-A-GLANCE INFORMATION

Length: 10.4 miles

Configuration: Loop with 1.7-mile out-and-back (0.85 miles each way)

Aerobic difficulty: Moderately strenuous; the ridge road has several steep intervals.

Technical difficulty: Easy; all smooth dirt road except for one flat singletrack section

Scenery: Great views from Scully Ridge of Water Canyon, Lower Aliso Canyon, San Gabriel Mountains, Santa Ana Mountains

Trail traffic: Light to none

Riding time: 1–2 hours

Access: Park near Rolling M Ranch off Bane Canyon Drive. Day use for Chino Hills State Park is $3, payable at entrance station on Bane Canyon Drive. Open Nov. 1–Mar. 31, 7 a.m.–6 p.m.; Apr. 1–Oct. 31, 7 a.m.–9 p.m.

Special comments: The parking area and the road near Rolling M Ranch are paved, but much of Bane Canyon Road is a graded dirt road. If you are adverse to getting your car dirty, I suggest starting the ride from the Bane Canyon turnoff at Sapphire Street (see Ride 4, Bane Canyon Loop). This will add about 6 miles to the ride.

GPS TRAILHEAD COORDINATES (WGS 84)

UTM Zone (WGS84) 11S
Easting 0434824
Northing 3753755
Latitude N 33°55'20"
Longitude W 117°42'18"

In Brief

From Bane Canyon Road follow the Lower Aliso Single-track to Lower Aliso Canyon Trail. After a short cruise, turn right on the Scully Ridge Trail and begin climbing. The trail follows the ridge, climbing in several steep intervals, and then finally drops down to the southern boundary of the park. Just before Green River Golf Course, head left on a singletrack and follow it, winding along the fence line, all the way to the bottom of Lower Aliso Canyon Trail. A smooth and gradual climb up Aliso Canyon returns you back to the trailhead.

Information

Chino Hills State Park
1879 Jackson Street
Riverside, CA 92504
(909) 780-6222
Note: the above address is nowhere near the trailhead.

Description

This ride is certainly not a downhiller's delight. The majority of the route follows well-worn dirt roads, and the downhill sections are neither challenging nor adrenaline inducing. However, this is a perfect ride for those who want a bit of solitude and an ample amount of exercise. In the southeastern part of Chino Hills State Park, Scully

DIRECTIONS

From the CA 5 and CA 55 interchange: Take CA 55 north 8 miles and merge onto CA 91 east. Go 11.9 miles and exit onto CA 71 (Corona Expressway) north. Follow CA 71 6.8 miles and exit at Soquel Canyon Parkway. Turn left on Soquel Canyon Parkway and continue 1.1 miles to Elinvar Drive. Turn left on Elinvar Drive and head uphill. After 0.2 miles, the road turns left and becomes Sapphire Street. The first right off Sapphire Street is Bane Canyon Drive. Head up Bane Canyon Drive 3.1 miles and turn left into the parking lot before you get to the Rolling M Ranch.

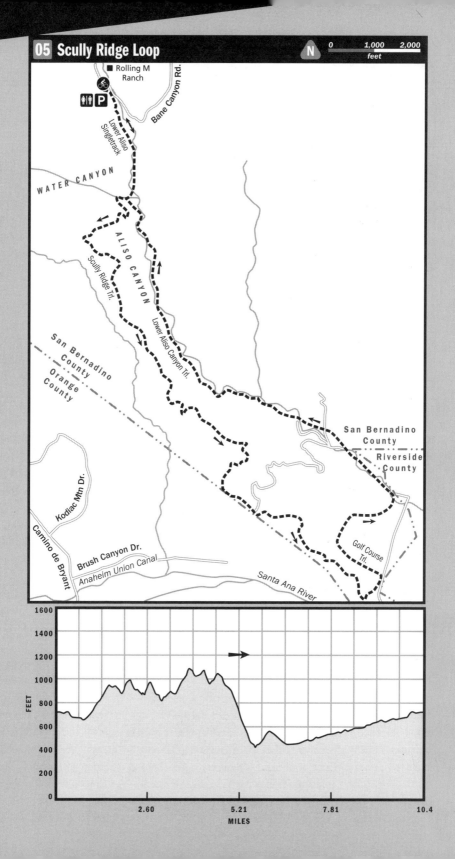

The matted grass terrain on Scully Ridge Road

Ridge runs from the Bane Canyon area all the way down the 91 freeway corridor. The trail, alternating between dirt road and doubletrack, barely sports enough traffic to keep from being reclaimed by grass and foliage. But it's not a rough trail—the surface is smooth and easily ridden. And the views are great, including a bird's-eye view of the 91 freeway: you'll be glad you're out riding and not commuting to the Inland Empire.

Begin on the paved section of Bane Canyon Road, riding away from the Rolling M Ranch. After just 0.1 mile, veer off on the Lower Aliso Singletrack, a connector trail to the Lower Aliso Canyon Trail. At 0.5 miles turn right on Lower Aliso Canyon Trail and head down the broad canyon.

Near 0.9 miles the road cuts right across Water Canyon Creek. Just past the trees, fork right and begin climbing the Scully Ridge Trail. At the first switchback, you'll see the trail-head for the Water Canyon Trail. Water Canyon is one of the most scenic sections of Chino Hills State Park, but the trail is closed to bikes.

Continue climbing, switchbacking up the first climb. At 1.7 miles stay left, avoiding the dead-end utility road to the right. By the end of the second climb, you'll see what lies ahead—more climbs. The trail follows an undulating path along Scully Ridge, changing from a graded dirt road to a narrow doubletrack and back to a dirt road without any rhyme or reason. Several of the climbs are steep, and parts of the doubletrack may be overgrown with matted grass. Don't try this ride after any significant rain: the wet grass and the "greasy" dirt conditions will make the climbs difficult, equivalent to dragging a plow behind your bicycle.

Each climbing interval is followed by a rolling descent. Take time to enjoy the views.

A view of Lower Aliso Canyon from Scully Ridge

The San Gabriel Mountains rise to the northeast, the Prado Dam lies to the east, and the Santa Ana Mountains are to the south. Pristine Brush Canyon runs directly below the ridge to the west. Past 4.3 miles Scully Hill Trail forks left. This dirt road drops directly into Lower Aliso Canyon and provides an option for a shorter version of the loop. Continuing on the ridge, make the final climb to Scully Hill. This is the final viewpoint, a dramatic overlook of the 91 freeway. OK, it's not Machu Picchu, but be happy you're on a bike and not sitting in traffic.

Head downhill on the fire road, winding toward Green River Golf Course. At 5.1 miles stay right, avoiding a dead-end utility road. The descent ends at 5.5 miles, and before you reach a gate, veer left on the golf course singletrack (an unnamed singletrack designated as the Golf Course Trail on the accompanying map). This trail suffers from too much equestrian use, and the terrain problems are more annoying than challenging. Most, if not all, of the trail should be rideable, though. Follow the fence line past a horse pasture and Green River Golf Course. Near 6.6 miles the trail crosses a large, and generally dry, creek bed.

Just past the creek, turn left up the Lower Aliso Canyon Trail. The trail, a dirt road, runs wide and smooth. Since you've already done some hard climbing on the ridge, you can be satisfied with a stress-free return. The gentle climb up the canyon is easily managed in middle to large gears. Several side roads branch from the Lower Aliso Canyon Trail, but stay left at all the forks and remain on the main canyon road. At 9.9 miles turn left on the Lower Aliso Singletrack and follow the trail back to the trailhead.

Note: The best months for riding in the Chino Hills are October through May. The summer months can be freakishly hot and smoggy.

FULLERTON

06

THE FULLERTON LOOP

Length: 11 miles

Configuration: Loop

Aerobic difficulty: Moderate; many small climbs and drops make this a good training ride.

Technical difficulty: Easy to moderate; optional sections can add to the difficulty.

Exposure: More than a third of the ride is in the shade.

Scenery: Suburban parkland, craftsman homes, a golf course, and a dam

Trail traffic: Moderate to heavy; the trails are a popular after-work destination for locals.

Riding time: 1–1.5 hours

Access: Free parking is available in the courthouse parking lot at 1275 Berkeley Avenue.

Special comments: Since this is a suburban trail running across the grid of the city, there are many places to access the loop. The official trailhead is next to the courthouse, at the start of the Juanita Cooke Trail. The recommended direction for the loop is clockwise.

In Brief

This is a complicated route with plenty of turns and intersections. If you are riding the loop unguided and for the first time, be sure to study the directions carefully or bring them along. This shouldn't discourage you from taking the ride—it is a hoot, with plenty of added singletrack sections developed by a core of dedicated local riders. The ride begins on the Juanita Cooke Trail and connects via streets, railroad tracks, and parkways to the Hiltschner, Castlewood, Nora Kuttner, and Bud Turner trails.

Description

Ride from the parking lot and hook onto the Juanita Cooke Trail. This is a gentle warm-up. The tree-lined trail climbs slightly as it crosses Valley View Drive and Richmond Avenue. Just past Richmond Avenue, a short spur trail runs parallel to the main route high on the right shoulder and provides a fun diversion.

Drop down to the left at 0.8 miles and onto the Hiltschner Trail. Stay left at 1 mile and follow the trail through Hiltschner Park. Crank hard on this fun singletrack section, dipping and winding through the trees. The trail runs along a creek and then intersects Euclid Street. Near 1.7 miles cross Euclid Street, jog left, and rejoin the Hiltschner Trail. Gear down and, at 1.8 miles, head right, up a steep hill. The short hill ends at West Valley View Drive.

GPS TRAILHEAD COORDINATES (WGS 84)

UTM Zone (WGS84)   11S
Easting   0414380
Northing   3749210
Latitude   N 33°52'47"
Longitude   W 117°55'33"

DIRECTIONS

From the CA 5 and CA 55 interchange: Follow CA 5 northbound to CA 57 north. Go 4.8 miles and then head west on CA 91. After 2.8 miles, exit at Lemon Street. Follow the off-ramp 0.5 miles and turn right on South Harbor Boulevard. Continue 1.1 miles and bear right on North Harbor Boulevard. After 0.6 miles, turn left on Berkeley Avenue. You'll see the courthouse on the left. The trailhead is at the south end of the courthouse parking lot.

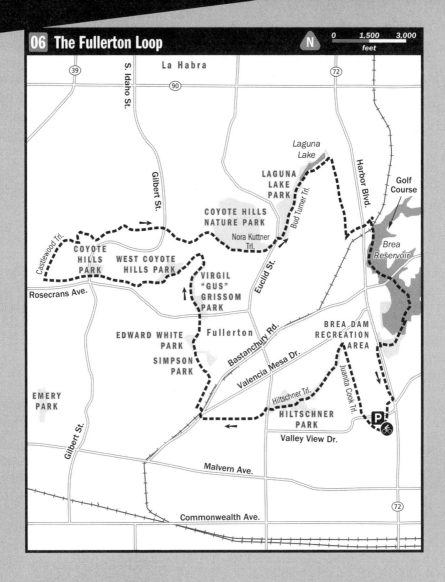

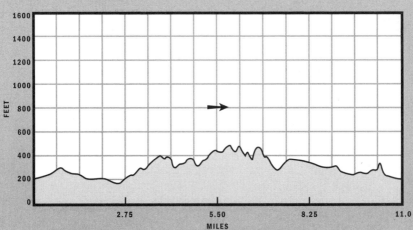

Follow the paved road, stay to the left of the median (the most direct route), and head straight through a stop sign. Turn right on Bastanchury Road, then left on Warburton Way. At 2.3 miles head right and follow a dirt trail on the right side of the railroad tracks. Cross North Parks Road at 2.6 miles and follow the dirt trail that parallels the street. This is the beginning of a gradual climb. Cross Rosecrans Avenue at 3.1 miles and ride up a paved trail through Virgil "Gus" Grissom Park. Veer right on a dirt doubletrack just past 3.5 miles and follow it along a property line. Cross Parks Road and stay high and to the left. Follow the singletrack as it roller coasters along and then plummets down to the main trail at 4.1 miles.

The trail runs up to, and then joins, a sidewalk. Veer left at 4.2 miles and stay on the sidewalk as it runs parallel to Rosecrans Avenue. Cross Gilbert Street at 4.6 miles and continue straight. Cross Sunny Ridge Drive and, just past 4.9 miles, make a hard right and begin climbing up the Castlewood Trail. The trail has a few options: take the far left fork and crank up a fence-line singletrack, winding through a tight section of trees. Climb to a culvert and then bound down over the ruts and roots back to the main trail.

The Castlewood Trail continues climbing to the highest point on the loop. Clear days will allow for views of Palos Verdes, Catalina Island, and Mount Baldy. Past the viewpoint, the trail drops, climbs, and then drops steeply to an intersection with Gilbert Street. Cross the street and stay on dirt as the trail parallels Castlewood Street.

Turn left on the Nora Kuttner Trail at 6.5 miles and grind uphill. At the top of the hill, head right on a singletrack and start downhill. The trail widens to a doubletrack, running fast and steep to Euclid Street. Turn left on Euclid Street and then take the first right at Laguna Road.

Make a quick left on the Bud Turner Trail and follow the singletrack straight across Clarion Road and all the way to Laguna Lake. Follow the dirt path on the right side of the lake, crossing Lakeside Drive. Turn right on the Juanita Cooke Trail at 8.1 miles. Crank past a gate, then charge up to the right at 8.3 miles and rip along a short singletrack diversion. Rejoin the main trail and keep riding to a bridge. At 8.6 miles turn sharply left and head downhill to the dirt path along the railroad tracks. The dirt trail finishes uphill intersecting a private road. Cross the pavement and follow the path along a golf course. Don't worry—the nets should protect you from any errant tee shots. Crank hard for maximum effect here. The trail winds and drops past two fairways and then ends at a series of parallel spillway tunnels. Head right, through the first tunnel.

Past the tunnel, the trail courses through a river bottom. There are several options, just be sure to pick one above the water line. Ride through the reeds and brush along the marshy waterway. At 10 miles head left and climb up behind the concrete dam. When you reach the concrete basin, stay on dirt and keep climbing. You'll reach the top of the climb near 10.2 miles; veer right here and then fork left to a steep section of singletrack. The trail plummets into a grassy roadside park. The drop is steep and silty, so watch out for other park users as you careen down toward the grass.

Cross the lawn toward Harbor Boulevard and head left. At 10.7 miles turn left on Valley View Drive and then take the first left on Berkeley Avenue. Crank down Berkeley Avenue to complete the loop.

The highest point on the trail

After the Ride

You'll find plenty of places to nosh in nearby downtown Fullerton. Try the Stadium Tavern, just off Harbor Boulevard. You can sit outside if you want to avoid the TV racket. The atmosphere is neighborhood sports bar with plenty of beers on tap and friendly servers. The food is healthy and hearty, certainly a class above normal bar food.

Stadium Tavern
305 North Harbor Boulevard
Fullerton, CA 92832
(714) 447-4200

ORANGE HILLS

PETERS CANYON

KEY AT-A-GLANCE INFORMATION

Length: 5.1 miles

Configuration: Double loop

Aerobic difficulty: Easy to moderate; the climbs are steep but quite short.

Technical difficulty: Easy

Exposure: Mostly complete sun

Scenery: Suburban backcountry— a man-made lake, some nonnative trees, and plenty of rooftops.

Trail traffic: Moderate to heavy; the small park is popular with runners and hikers.

Riding time: 1 hour or less

Access: Parking is available in the dirt lot near the trailhead. Bring three dollar bills for the parking machine. The trailhead is on the west side of the parking lot.

Special comments: The park is popular with runners, hikers, and families. There are a limited number of trails, so beware of congestion. The short loop around the upper reservoir is a great ride for kids.

In Brief

There are three primary trails in Peters Canyon Regional Park: Lakeview Trail, Lower Canyon Trail, and East Ridge Trail. East Ridge and Lower Canyon trails run parallel; a couple of decent singletracks connect the two routes.

This loop follows the Lakeview Trail around the west side of the reservoir and then drops down the length of the Lower Canyon Trail. From the far end of the Lower Canyon Trail, a singletrack winds up to the East Ridge Trail. The route back includes a series of short, steep climbs and subsequent drops along the East Ridge. The last climb leads back to the Lakeview Trail. A short jaunt around the east side of the lake completes the loop.

Alternatively, you could begin on the Lakeview Trail, climb immediately to the East Ridge, and then drop down to the Lower Canyon Trail on the Sage singletrack or the East Ridge singletrack. Then it is an easy ride up the Lower Canyon Trail back to the Lakeview Trail. This alternate loop offers a better, albeit short, downhill, but also one heck of a steep climb at the north end of the East Ridge.

Information

Peters Canyon Regional Park
8548 East Canyon View Avenue
Orange, CA 92869
(714) 973-6611 or (714) 973 6612
peterscanyon@ocparks.com

GPS TRAILHEAD COORDINATES (WGS 84)
UTM Zone (WGS84) 11S
Easting 0429401
Northing 3738462
Latitude N 33°47'02"
Longitude W 117°45'45"

DIRECTIONS

From the CA 5 and CA 55 freeway interchange: Go north on CA 55 3 miles and exit at Chapman Avenue East. Follow the off-ramp 0.2 miles and turn right on Chapman Avenue. Follow Chapman Avenue 4.4 miles and turn right on Jamboree Road. After 0.5 miles, turn right on Canyon View Avenue, take the first left on Old Camp Road, and park.

From the CA 5 freeway: exit at Jamboree Road. Head north for 5.3 miles, turn left on Canyon View Avenue, take the first left on Old Camp Road, and park.

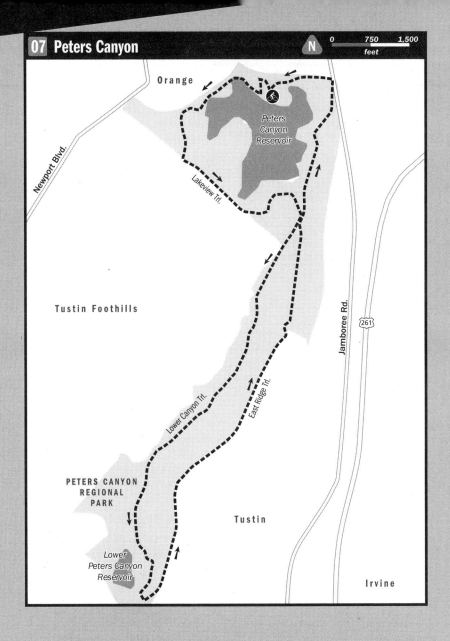

N

0   750   1,500
feet

Orange

Peters
Canyon
Reservoir

Lakeview Trl.

Newport Blvd.

Jamboree Rd.

261

Tustin Foothills

East Ridge Trl.

Lower Canyon Trl.

PETERS CANYON
REGIONAL
PARK

Tustin

Lower
Peters Canyon
Reservoir

Irvine

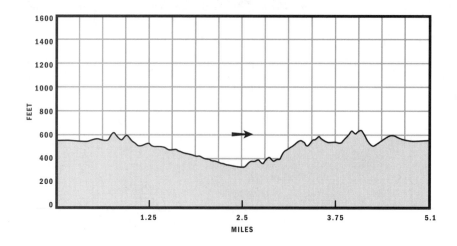

Description

Follow the Lakeview Trail toward the west side of the lake. The trail winds through reeds and brush near the water's edge. The course is narrow but serviceably smooth and flat. Be on the lookout for hikers and bird-watchers—park users of all types and ages frequent this section. Near 0.4 miles head right, following the Lakeview Trail away from the lake and toward an adjacent housing tract. At 0.7 miles a short climb leads to perhaps the best view-point on the trail. You can look down on the lake, actually a reservoir, and eye some of the local wildlife. The wetlands are an essential habitat for migrating waterfowl.

At 1 mile, just past a second short climb, veer right and follow a narrow path into Peters Canyon. The drop has plenty of silt but is easily managed. The trail fans out onto a dirt road at the bottom. Continue downhill on the road. On the left side of the canyon, you will see the steep hill that leads to the East Ridge. Unless you intend to do the alternate version of the loop, stay to the right, heading slightly downhill. The Lower Canyon Trail runs along a narrow gap between the East Ridge and a residential area. A few connector trails lead up to the ridge. Another short singletrack runs through the trees, parallel to the road, before it veers off into the adjacent housing development. Any of these trails are options if you wish to explore or add a bit of distance to the short loop.

At 2.6 miles the Lower Canyon Trail ends at a metal gate. Beyond the gate is the lower reservoir, a concrete flood-control channel. A paved bike path begins at the gate, following the channel to Jamboree Road.

Stay on the dirt, veering left at the gate onto a narrow trail. This is arguably the most scenic part of the ride. The trail winds through a grove of eucalyptus trees, climbing, traversing, and switchbacking up to the East Ridge. The trail clears the trees at the ridgeline, allowing for an uninspired view of a housing tract. Forget the view and follow the doubletrack along the ridge. This is where the bulk of the climbing occurs. The trail drops and climbs in three successive intervals. All of the climbs are short—but they are steep, and loose dirt and rocks make them a challenge to clean. At 3.9 miles stay right, following the East Ridge Trail

42

Picnic benches near the water

as it continues to climb. The trail narrows to a singletrack and ascends to the highest point in the park. Once you reach the picnic bench, it's straight downhill to the canyon.

Just past 4.3 miles keep to the right and make the short and forgiving climb up to the east shore of the lake. Follow the trail around the lake until it dead-ends at a gate. At 4.9 miles step through the gate and turn left. The trail momentarily parallels Canyon View Avenue and then cuts back into the brush. Spin the last 100 yards through the tall reeds until you arrive back at the parking lot.

After the Ride

Head north on Jamboree Road back to Chapman Avenue. You'll find CJ Coffee House in the shopping center next to Albertsons. Sit outdoors and pretend you are in a café somewhere other than in a strip mall. The food is basic, mostly cold sandwiches, but it's consistently good. They also have sumptuous pastries and cookies.

CJ Coffeehouse
8512 East Chapman Avenue
Orange, CA 92869
(714) 639-7705

08

WEIR CANYON
(SANTIAGO OAKS)

Length: 12.1 miles

Configuration: Double loop

Aerobic difficulty: Moderate to strenuous; one extended climb and several short climbs

Technical difficulty: Moderate; The Chutes is a fun and somewhat technical downhill; remainder of ride is not technical.

Exposure: Complete sun

Scenery: Nice backcountry amid suburban sprawl; great views from the ridgeline of the Orange County basin and Chino Hills State Park

Trail traffic: Moderate overall; Santiago Creek is popular with equestrians; less traffic in Weir Canyon

Riding time: 1.5–2.25 hours

Access: Parking in nearby Irvine Regional Park is $3 weekdays and $5 weekends. Most weekdays there is no attendant, and you will need 3 fairly crisp dollar bills for the parking machine. Free parking may be available on nearby streets.

Special comments: The route follows trails in Santiago Creek, Santiago Oaks, and Weir Canyon regional parks.

GPS TRAILHEAD
COORDINATES (WGS 84)

UTM Zone (WGS84)   11S
Easting   0429542
Northing   3739893
Latitude   N 33°47'45"
Longitude   W 117°45'40"

In Brief

Ride the length of Santiago Creek Trail and push up three consecutive climbs on the Anaheim Hills Trail. Drop down the Weir Canyon Trail and follow the rolling doubletrack to Hidden Canyon Road. A short climb on the street leads to the Lower Canyon Loop in Weir Canyon Regional Park. After numerous climbs and drops through Weir Canyon, climb back up to the Anaheim Hills Ridge. Head south on The Chutes, following the rough-and-tumble singletrack all the way to Santiago Creek. A couple of flat dirt roads lead through the creek basin back to the trailhead.

Information

Irvine Regional Park
1 Irvine Park Road
Orange, CA 92862
(714) 973-6823

Description

The directions for this route may seem complicated on paper, but they are actually easy to follow. With only a couple of exceptions, you can navigate most of the ride

DIRECTIONS

From the CA 5 and CA 55 freeway interchange: Go north on CA 55 3 miles and exit at Chapman Avenue East. Follow the off-ramp 0.2 miles and turn right on Chapman Avenue. Follow Chapman Avenue for 4.4 miles and turn left on Jamboree Road. Continue another 0.2 miles and, at road's end, turn right, into the park. Once inside the park, turn left at the gate and park in the Group 4 lot. The trailhead is near the park entrance, at the end of Jamboree Road.

From CA 5 freeway: Exit at Jamboree Road and head north for 5.9 miles. Turn right into the park just after you cross Santiago Canyon Road. Once inside the park, turn left at the gate and park in the Group 4 lot. The trailhead is near the park entrance, at the end of Jamboree Road.

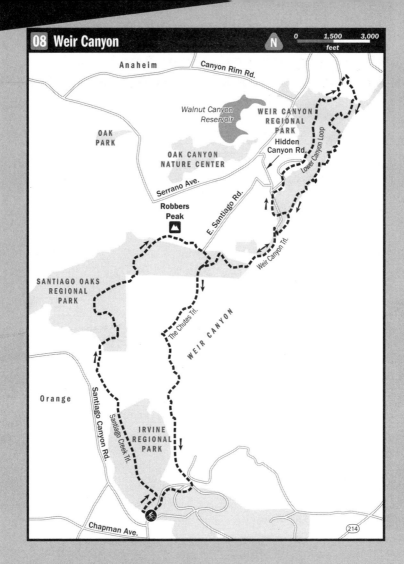

N

0   1,500   3,000
feet

Anaheim   Canyon Rim Rd.

Walnut Canyon
Reservoir

WEIR CANYON
REGIONAL
PARK

OAK
PARK

OAK CANYON
NATURE CENTER

Hidden
Canyon Rd.

Lower Canyon Loop

Serrano Ave.

Robbers
Peak

E. Santiago Rd.

Weir Canyon Trl.

SANTIAGO OAKS
REGIONAL
PARK

The Chutes Trl.

WEIR CANYON

Orange

Santiago Canyon Rd.

Santiago Creek Trl.

IRVINE
REGIONAL
PARK

Chapman Ave.

214

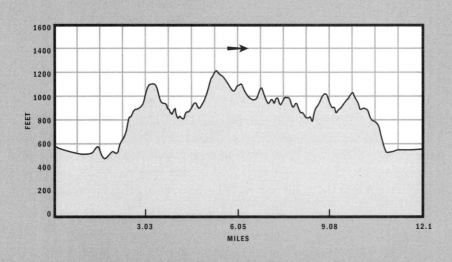

1600				
1400				
1200				
1000				
800				
600				
400				
200				
0				

FEET

3.03   6.05   9.08   12.1

MILES

Looking down the first climb

by dead reckoning: your instincts, a general understanding of the route, and a few key geographical markers will guide you.

Begin on the Santiago Creek Trail. As of this writing, the trail detours due to a nearby construction project. When the detour is removed, there may be minor changes to the overall mileage. Ride down the dirt doubletrack, following it northward through the river bottom. It's an easy ride and a great warm-up before the hill climbs—just keep an eye out for equestrians.

At 1.4 miles veer left and climb a gravel road. At the top of the hill, stay right on a paved road. The road continues toward the dam. Near 1.5 miles follow the sign to Santiago Oaks Regional Park and turn left down the steep dirt road. Turn right at the bottom of the hill on another dirt road. Follow that road, staying on the north side of the dam and heading toward the hills. At 1.9 miles turn right on the Sage Hill Trail and prepare to climb. The next mile-plus consists of three consecutive steep grades. After each successive climb, the road passes through a gate. There's no need to worry about directions, though. Just stay on the road, crank hard, and keep going up. The last section of the climb follows a gravel road.

At 3.4 miles turn right on pavement and head toward a utility tower. Follow the connector trail to the left of the tower, dropping down slightly. Past 3.6 miles make a sharp switchback left and head down the Weir Canyon Trail. This doubletrack-cum-fire road drops sharply and then climbs in several intervals. Just keep following the signs for Weir Canyon. At 4.5 miles turn right and downhill; then, before a gate, turn left up a singletrack. Get in a small gear, because the trail climbs steeply. Push hard to the top of the hill, then fork left and coast down to pavement.

Continue straight on Hidden Canyon Road and then make the first right on East Santiago Road. The street ends at Weir Canyon Regional Park. Veer left on the dirt and continue climbing. Push along the dirt road, riding toward the northern boundary of the park. The road follows a rolling ridge and then heads down into Weir Canyon—dropping, climbing, and then dropping again and again in succession. This is certainly a ride you'll do faster and faster on successive attempts. The course is full of tight turns, and it is difficult to anticipate some of the short climbs. Nevertheless, the trail is fun, scenic, and relatively untrammeled.

After you complete the Weir Canyon Loop, continue straight at 8.2 miles and retrace the Weir Canyon Trail. The final climb comes at 8.9 miles, as you return to Santiago Oaks Regional Park. At 9.6 miles, instead of climbing back to the utility tower, turn left on the ridgeline singletrack. Stay on the ridgeline, following the narrow, troughlike trail. It's a fast, smooth ride with only a couple of minor rock sections. Veer right at 9.8 miles. Then, past 10.3 miles, take the second left down The Chutes. The most technical section comes immediately—a steep channel through smooth rocks and ruts. Continuing downhill, the trail traverses the hillside, winding between brush and occasional clumps of cactus. The singletrack rolls out near the Santiago Creek basin. Ride south across a creek bed and then head straight onto a dirt road. There are a few options here, because various roads criss-cross Santiago Creek. Just keep heading south, following the obvious route toward Irvine Regional Park. Before you reach the park, a road cuts back to the trailhead to complete the loop.

Note: The Anaheim Hills Trail lies in an unnamed open space. Pay careful attention to the route descriptions and the trail signs as not to veer into the adjacent private land holdings.

After the Ride

By all means go to Taco Mesa. If you haven't been, don't question. Just go. The casual restaurant has sumptuous offerings with plenty of variety and nuance. Short of Santa Barbara's La Superica, this is probably the best Taco Stand in Southern California.

Taco Mesa

3533 East Chapman Avenue

Orange, CA 92869-3854

(714) 633-3932

SANTA ANA MOUNTAINS

THE LUGE

Length: 7.4 miles

Configuration: Loop

Aerobic difficulty: Moderate; the ride is short, and the climbing is evenly distributed.

Technical difficulty: Variable; no full-blown technical sections on the route, but The Luge is a challenging downhill for those who want to push and go fast.

Exposure: Complete sun with only bits of shade

Scenery: Views of the Saddleback Valley and beyond; the Vulture Crags rock formation is definitely a highlight.

Trail traffic: Light to moderate; riders from nearby Whiting Ranch Regional Park may add to the crowds on weekends.

Riding time: 1–1.25 hours

Access: Free parking is available in the parking lot near Cook's Corner. The adjacent restaurant, a popular hangout for bikers (the nonpeddling variety), is extremely busy on weekends. Park on the dirt to avoid conflicts with the restaurant owners. Most of the ride takes place in the Cleveland National Forest.

GPS TRAILHEAD COORDINATES (WGS 84)

UTM Zone (WGS84)   11S
Easting   0442601
Northing   3727315
Latitude   N 33°41'03"
Longitude   W 117°37'09"

In Brief

This is a relatively small loop within a large wilderness area. Begin on pavement, following Santiago Canyon Road to the Modjeska Grade. Grind up Modjeska Grade for 0.5 miles and turn right onto the Santiago Trail. The trail, a mix of singletrack and fire road, climbs along the ridge above Modjeska Canyon. After a short downhill stretch, turn onto the Luge Trail and charge downhill. The Luge isn't steep, but it has enough rocks, ruts, and tight turns to make it challenging. At the bottom of the trail, a short unnamed road takes you back to Live Oak Canyon Road. From the road, a straight shot downhill ends at the parking lot.

Description

This ride is short and can easily be accomplished in an hour. However, it is a damn good hour. A high-quality ride with plenty of scenic vistas and a challenging downhill, this loop is especially good for those who don't have the legs or the time to make the longer climbs to the top of Saddleback. And for those who want a bit more, this ride can easily be combined with a loop through Whiting Ranch.

DIRECTIONS

From the intersection of the CA 405 freeway and the CA 133 freeway: Head south on CA 405 1.4 miles and exit at Bake Parkway (Exit 1B). Turn left on Bake Parkway, go 5.3 miles, and turn right on Portola Parkway. After 0.7 miles, turn left on Glenn Ranch Road. Go 1.6 miles and turn left on El Toro Road. At 2 miles, where El Toro Road becomes Santiago Canyon Road, look for Cook's Corner. Just before the restaurant, turn right on Live Oak Canyon Road and then left into the parking lot.

From the intersection of the CA 5 freeway and the CA 55 freeway: Go north on CA 55 for 3.2 miles and exit at Chapman Avenue. Turn right and then continue straight as Chapman Avenue becomes Santiago Canyon Road. At 15.1 miles from CA 55, you'll see Cook's Corner on the left. Just past Cook's Corner, turn left on Live Oak Canyon and then left into the parking lot.

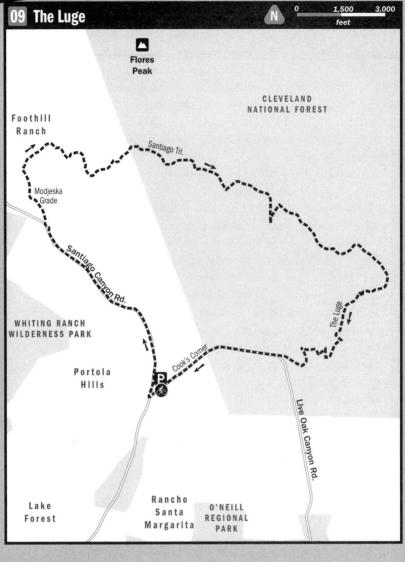

0   1,500   3,000
feet

Flores Peak

CLEVELAND
NATIONAL FOREST

Foothill
Ranch

Santiago Trl.

Modjeska
Grade

Santiago Canyon Rd.

WHITING RANCH
WILDERNESS PARK

The Luge

Portola
Hills

Cook's Corner

Live Oak Canyon Rd.

Lake
Forest

Rancho
Santa
Margarita

O'NEILL
REGIONAL
PARK

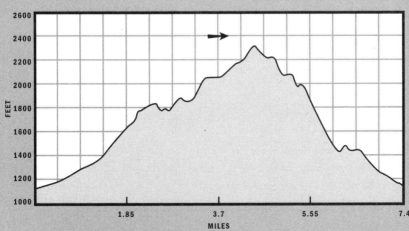

From Cook's Corner head right on Santiago Canyon Road. This is a busy and potentially dangerous road. Be careful when riding in groups, particularly on weekends and during commuting hours. On weekends, scores of motorcyclists cruise the road.

The climb on Santiago Canyon Road is mild but noticeable. After 1.3 miles turn right on another paved road, the Modjeska Grade. Shift down—there is a reason they call it the Modjeska *Grade*. The narrow road doesn't have a bike lane or a rideable shoulder. Fortunately, traffic is much lighter than on Santiago Canyon Road. Crank hard, and this section will be over before you know it.

At 1.8 miles turn right on the Santiago Trail—this is where the dirt section of ride begins. The Santiago Trail, alternately fire road and singletrack, climbs the ridgeline above Santiago and Modjeska canyons. The ascent is gradual, rolling along the ridge. Short, steep sections are interspersed with easy flat sections and short downhill sections. At 3.6 miles the path cuts to the Modjeska side of the ridge, allowing for unobstructed views of the canyon below and the Santa Ana Mountains above. The climb continues, topping out at near the 4.4-mile point, and then heads downhill along a stone-filled section of trail. The route levels temporarily just below Vulture Crags—knobby spires of sandstone that were once nesting grounds for California condors. The endangered condor no longer nests here, or in any other Orange County locale, but you may see a few turkey vultures or a lone raptor soaring above the crags.

Near 5 miles you'll notice a flagpole mounted on a small hill above the trail. This is a well-placed, although incidental, marker for the next part of the ride—The Luge. No need to climb to the flag: just continue past the mound and turn right on the trail.

The Luge courses along a narrow ridge to the canyon below. The trail isn't overtly technical and certainly not steep. However, the downhill is fun and challenging, particularly if you want to go fast. The path is slightly concave with small berms on either side. There are also collections of small stones and ruts—plenty of obstacles to keep you on edge. Push through the tight turns and bounce down the sequences of small, steplike drop-offs. This is a perfect trail to hone your riding skills.

At 6.1 miles The Luge bottoms out near a chain-link fence. Turn right and cross a small wooden bridge. Gear down, because just past the bridge, the trail climbs steeply for about 100 yards. After the short climb, at 6.2 miles, continue right and follow the trail to an unnamed private road. Turn left on the road and continue downhill. The road ends at a gate, but a small (yet obvious) trail cuts around the gate to Live Oak Canyon Road.

At 6.5 miles turn right on Live Oak Canyon Road. From here, a straight shot downhill leads to the parking lot. The road is steep and without a bike lane. Fortunately, traffic is light, and the steep grade allows you to travel as fast as the cars.

After the Ride

You're already there, so why not join the motor heads at the "world famous" Cook's Corner bar and restaurant. The old roadhouse is probably one of the Southland's most renowned biker bars. But don't worry, these days "bikers" tend to be weekenders who spend Monday through Friday working for Fortune 500 companies.

Cook's Corner, 19122 Live Oak Canyon Road
Trabuco Canyon, CA 92679 (949) 858-0266

10

SILVERADO MOTORWAY LOOP

KEY AT-A-GLANCE INFORMATION

Length: 16.6 miles

Configuration: Loop with 0.4-mile out-and-back (0.2 miles each way)

Aerobic difficulty: Fairly difficult; although easier than most other Santa Ana Mountain rides

Technical difficulty: Moderate plus; the motorway isn't steep, but it has plenty of fist-sized rocks. Charging down the entire trail requires more stamina than skill.

Exposure: Mostly complete sun

Scenery: The gamut of the Cleveland National Forest: riparian wilderness in the canyon, subalpine splendor on the ridgetop, and plenty of chaparral-laden hillsides in between

Trail traffic: Moderate

Riding time: 2–3.5 hours

Access: Park in the lot at the base of Maple Springs Road. An Adventure Pass is required to park near the trailhead. Daily and annual passes may be purchased on the U.S. Forest Service Web site or at local sporting-goods stores such as Sportmart, Sport Chalet, and Big 5. Check the Forest Service Web site for a dealer near you.

GPS TRAILHEAD COORDINATES (WGS 84)

UTM Zone (WGS84) 11S
Easting 0445948
Northing 3734314
Latitude N 33°44'51"
Longitude W 117°35'01"

In Brief

Crank up the length of Maple Springs Road. After 7-plus miles, turn left on Main Divide Road. Follow the rolling ridge road another 6 miles to the top of Silverado Motorway. The way down is fast and rocky—all singletrack. The motorway bottoms out at Maple Springs Road. Retrace Maple Springs Road a short distance back to the trailhead.

Information

Cleveland National Forest—Trabuco Ranger District
Keith Fletcher, District Ranger
1147 East Sixth Street
Corona, CA 92879
(951) 736-1811

Description

Every serious (or even halfway serious) Orange County mountain biker should ride the Santa Ana Mountains. No other local riding area can match the Santa Ana's remoteness, majestic scenery, and shear scale. It's the only

DIRECTIONS

From the intersection of the CA 405 freeway and the CA 133 freeway: Head south on CA 405 1.4 miles and exit at Bake Parkway (Exit 1B). Turn left on Bake Parkway, go 5.3 miles, and turn right on Portola Parkway. After 0.7 miles turn left on Glenn Ranch Road. Go 1.6 miles and turn left on El Toro Road. After 2 miles, at Cook's Corner, El Toro becomes Santiago Canyon Road. Continue another 5.8 miles to Silverado Canyon. Turn right on Silverado Canyon Road and go 5.7 miles. There is a parking area next to the road's end turnabout.

From the intersection of the CA 5 freeway and the CA 55 freeway: Go north on CA 55 3.2 miles and exit at Chapman Avenue. Turn right and continue straight as Chapman Avenue becomes Santiago Canyon Road. At 9.3 miles from CA 55, turn left on Silverado Canyon Road and follow it 5.7 miles to its end. There is a parking area next to the road's end turnabout.

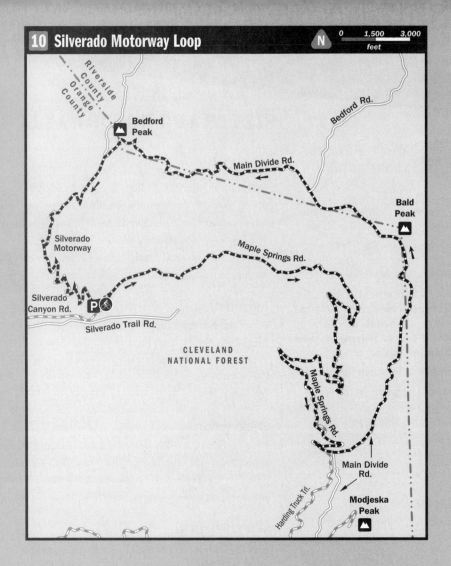

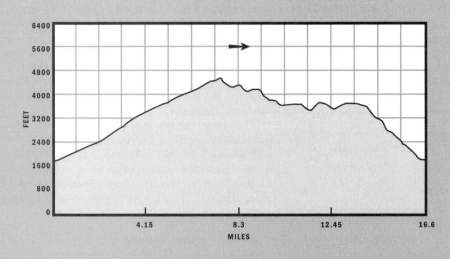

place in Orange County where mountain biking actually means climbing mountains . . . and descending mountains.

If you've never ridden in the Santa Anas, this loop might be a good place to start. There are certainly easier rides in the area. Out-and-back rides on Blackstar Canyon Road, Maple Springs Road, or Harding Truck Trail allow you to ride out as far as you wish, then turn tail and head home. However, if you're goal oriented and want to push yourself, a loop ride is always a better option. Without adding much more effort to the Maple Springs climb, this route gives you a full-scale Santa Ana Mountain experience and a fun singletrack descent to boot.

Maple Springs Road begins where Silverado Canyon Road ends. The gate at the trailhead is generally (if not always) open, allowing access for trucks and motorcycles. Ride up Maple Springs Road, which is paved for the first 3 miles as it courses through the upper reaches of Silverado Canyon. The climb is gradual at the start, allowing for ample warm-up. After the pavement ends, the road ascends above the canyon in a series of long switchbacks. Mostly it's a long, steady climb on fairly smooth dirt. Good climbers will be able to crank in the middle chainring, shifting down or standing up for a couple of short, steeper sections.

Near the top of the ascent, the Harding Truck Trail merges with Maple Springs Road. Continue straight through a gate at 7.1 miles. At 7.2 miles turn left on Main Divide Road. Main Divide Road runs predominantly downhill as it wraps around the east side of Silverado Canyon. You'll have nice views of your ascent route on the left, and better views of the San Bernardino Mountains, Lake Matthews, and the CA 15 corridor on the right.

Try to keep your speed on the downhills and use momentum to push up the short ensuing climbs. Be mindful of other users, including trucks and motorcycles. Be ready for sudden bumpy, rutty, and loose sections on the road. You don't want to crash this far from home.

At 10.8 miles Bedford Road veers right and heads down to the Corona area; bear left here and stay on the ridge. After 11 miles the road climbs steeply, rising 300 feet in about 0.4 miles. This ascent is followed by a steep downhill and then one final climb to Bedford Peak. After you crest the peak, at 13.3 miles, look for the Silverado Motorway trailhead on your left.

The Motorway initially cuts a wide ridgetop path away from Main Divide Road. Stay on the left side of the ridge—after a short climb the trail narrows and becomes increasingly rocky. The riding isn't technically difficult, but fast descents will prove fun and challenging. Veer left and downhill near 14.3 miles, at the junction with the Ladd Ridge Trail.

Charge down the rest of the Silverado Motorway. The trail switchbacks down the steep canyon wall. Hang on and stay on the trail. By the time you complete the jarring 2-mile descent, you'll be shaken . . . but not stirred. At trail's end, turn right on Maple Springs Road and make an easy return to the parking lot.

After the Ride

Stop at Silverado Café. In the morning get their no-frills pancakes; in the afternoon and evening enjoy the all-you-can-eat buffet. Even better, draught beers are only $1 with the buffet.

Silverado Café
28272 Silverado Canyon Road
Silverado, CA
(714) 649-2622

11

SANTIAGO PEAK

KEY AT-A-GLANCE INFORMATION

Length: 23.6 miles

Configuration: Out-and-back

Aerobic difficulty: Fairly difficult; a long, mostly gradual, climb

Technical difficulty: Easy to moderate; fire road with a couple of rocky sections

Exposure: Full sun with sporadic shade. First 3 miles are shadiest.

Scenery: Stunning views from the top of Orange County

Trail traffic: Light to moderate

Riding time: 2.75–4.25 hours

Access: Parking near the trailhead requires an Adventure Pass. Daily and annual passes may be purchased on the U.S. Forest Service Web site or at sporting goods shops such as Sportmart, Big 5, and Sport Chalet.

Special comments: Maple Springs Road and Main Divide Road are open to vehicular traffic. Recreational traffic is greatest on weekends and generally more concentrated on Maple Springs Road. You may encounter service vehicles weekdays on either road. Keep your ears open and, wherever possible, stay on the right side of the road.

GPS TRAILHEAD COORDINATES (WGS 84)

UTM Zone (WGS84) 11S

Easting 0445948

Northing 3734314

Latitude N 33°44'51"

Longitude W 117°35'01"

In Brief

Climb the length of Maple Springs Road to the Main Divide. Turn right on Main Divide Road and continue the ascent. You'll pass the turnoff to Modjeska Peak near 8.7 miles. At this point the route to Santiago Peak will be in clear view. Follow the final switchbacks along Main Divide Road all the way to the highest point in the Santa Ana Mountains—5,687 feet. The return ride is completely downhill, save one minor climb near Modjeska Peak.

Description

Climb to the top of the hill and ride down. This is the elementary principle, the crux, the cornerstone of all mountain biking activity. In this case the hill happens to be Santiago Peak—the highest point in Orange County. If that doesn't sound like much, remember, that at 5,687 feet, Modjeska Peak rises higher than any point in 31 of the lower 48 states. If your friends in Maine, New Hampshire, Vermont, or North Dakota claim they are riding big hills, tell them you are going higher. Sure there

DIRECTIONS

From the intersection of the CA 405 freeway and CA 133: Head south on CA 405 1.4 miles and exit at Bake Parkway (Exit 1B). Turn left on Bake Parkway, go 5.3 miles, and turn right on Portola Parkway. After 0.7 miles turn left on Glenn Ranch Road. Go 1.6 miles and turn left on El Toro Road. After 2 miles, at Cook's Corner, El Toro becomes Santiago Canyon Road. Continue another 5.8 miles to Silverado Canyon Road. Turn right on Silverado Canyon Road and go 5.7 miles. There is a parking area next to the road's end turnabout (this is the beginning of Maple Springs Road).

   From the intersection of the CA 5 freeway and CA 55: Go north on CA 55 3.2 miles and exit at Chapman Avenue. Turn right and continue straight as Chapman Avenue becomes Santiago Canyon Road. At 9.3 miles from CA 55, turn left on Silverado Canyon Road and follow it 5.7 miles to its end. There is a parking area next the road's end turnabout.

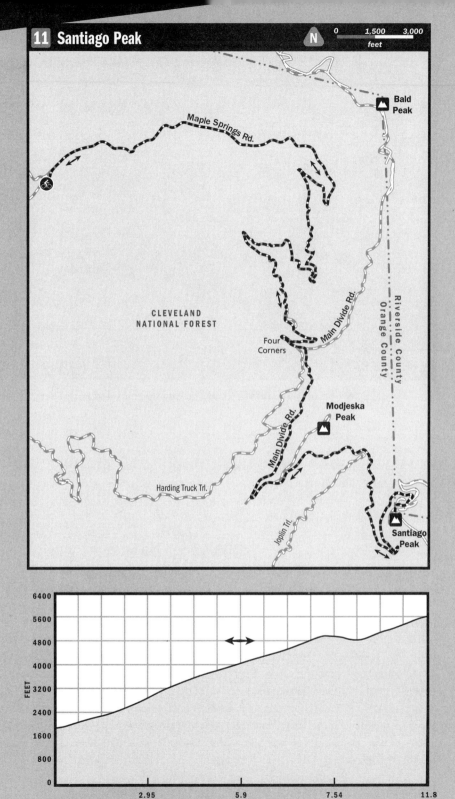

A rocky section of Main Divide Road, looking back toward Four Corners

are plenty of taller peaks in California—much taller—but Santiago Peak is on your home turf, and it's a great ride.

Crank up Maple Springs Road. The first section is paved, running parallel to a lush creek bed. At 3 miles the road hairpins right and becomes dirt. Strong riders should be able to push the middle chainring up much of the climb. The grade rises evenly, with only a couple of steeper pushes, as it switchbacks up to the divide.

Near 6.9 miles continue straight through a white metal gate toward Four Corners—the confluence of Maple Springs Road, Harding Truck Trail, and Main Divide Road. At 7.2 miles continue a few feet past the Harding Truck Trail and turn right on Main Divide Road. The dirt road runs south, then southeast, as it wraps around Modjeska Peak. Near 8 miles a carpet of loose rocks makes for tough going. Keep your momentum and push around the lower peak; you'll reach the turnoff to Modjeska Peak at 8.8 miles. Bear right—the road runs gradually downhill before making the final push to Santiago Peak. The Joplin Trail drops steeply to the right at 9.6 miles. Downhill in the distance, you can see the clearing for Old Camp.

The final section of the climb switchbacks up, then wraps around the top of, Santiago Peak. At 11.6 miles, just after you pass a canopy of trees, you'll reach the turnoff for the peak. Turn right and make the short ride up to a set of signal towers. Find a shady spot and enjoy the view—because of the towers and the trees, the best views are to the south, the southwest, and the west. Clear days will allow for bird's-eye views of Catalina and San Clemente islands, the Saddleback Valley, coastal Orange County, and maybe your house.

When you're finished resting, the way back, a simple retrace, is easy and obvious. The entire route runs downhill, aside from the minor push around Modjeska Peak.

KEY AT-A-GLANCE INFORMATION

Length: 22.5 miles

Configuration: Shuttle ride

Aerobic difficulty: Fairly difficult; a long, mostly gradual, climb

Technical difficulty: Moderate plus; taking the option to ride down the Upper Holy Jim Trail will make the ride more technical.

Exposure: Varied; most of the shade comes on the descent.

Scenery: A virtual buffet of views and vistas from the Main Divide; lush hillside and canyon greenery on the Holy Jim Trail

Trail traffic: Light to moderate; watch for vehicular traffic on the climb and hikers on the descent.

Riding time: 3.5–5 hours

Access: Parking near the trailhead requires an Adventure Pass. Daily and annual passes may be purchased on the U.S. Forest Service Web site or from local sporting-goods shops such as Big 5 and Sport Chalet. Parking at the endpoint is free. Parking on the upper portion of Trabuco Creek Road (in Cleveland National Forest) requires an Adventure Pass.

Special comments: Maple Springs Road and the Main Divide Road are open to vehicular traffic. Recreational traffic is greatest on weekends and generally more concentrated on Maple Springs Road. You may encounter service vehicles weekdays on either road. Keep your ears open and, where possible, stay on the right side of the road.

MAPLE SPRINGS TO HOLY JIM SHUTTLE RIDE

In Brief

Climb the length of Maple Springs Road to the Main Divide. Turn right on Main Divide Road and continue climbing as the rock-strewn road courses around Modjeska Peak. After a modest downhill, cut left on the Saddle Trail and climb to the back side of Santiago Peak. Reconnect with Main Divide Road about 200 feet below the peak. The rest of the ride runs completely downhill. At 11.5 miles you may either fork onto the steep and technical Upper Holy Jim

DIRECTIONS TO THE ENDPOINT

From the intersection of the CA 405 freeway and CA 133: Head south on CA 405 1.4 miles and exit at Bake Parkway (Exit 1B). Turn left on Bake Parkway, go 5.3 miles, and turn right on Portola Parkway. After 0.7 miles turn left on Glenn Ranch Road. Go 1.6 miles and turn left on El Toro Road. After 2 miles, at Cook's Corner, El Toro becomes Santiago Canyon Road. Here, turn right on Live Oak Canyon and go 4.3 miles to Trabuco Creek Road. (It's just after Rose Canyon Drive.) Park your first car on the dirt shoulder near the intersection of Trabuco Creek Road and Live Oak Canyon Drive.

From the intersection of the CA 5 freeway and CA 55: Go north on CA 55 3.2 miles and exit at Chapman Avenue. Turn right on Chapman Avenue and continue straight as Chapman Avenue becomes Santiago Canyon Road. At 15.1 miles from CA 55, you'll see Cook's Corner on the left. Turn left on Live Oak Canyon Road and go 4.3 miles to Trabuco Creek Road. (It's just after Rose Canyon Drive.) Park your first car on the dirt shoulder near the intersection of Trabuco Creek Road and Live Oak Canyon Drive.

DIRECTIONS TO THE STARTING POINT

From the intersection of Trabuco Creek and Live Oak Canyon roads: Return on Live Oak Canyon Road 4.3 miles to Cook's Corner. Turn right on Santiago Canyon Road and go 5.8 miles to Silverado Canyon Road. Turn right on Silverado Canyon Road and drive 5.4 miles up the canyon to a gate. Park your second car in the adjacent lot (but do not block the gate).

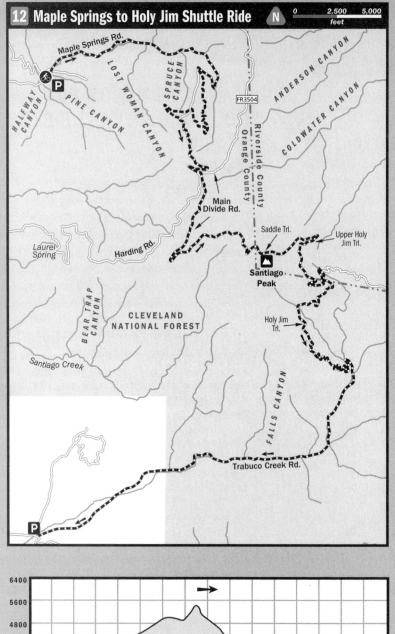

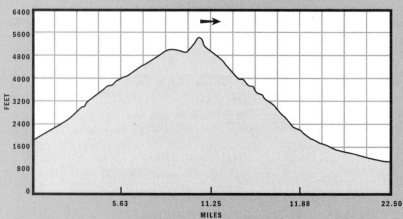

Trail or continue on down the divide to the main section of the Holy Jim Trail. The ride down Holy Jim Trail is beautiful and outrageously fun. Follow the cascading singletrack down the face of Santiago Peak, ripping around switchbacks and across streams all the way to Trabuco Creek Road. Crank the length of Trabuco Creek to finish the ride.

Description

Shuttle rides, particularly with large groups of riders, can be time consuming and logistically complicated. Nobody wants to spend more time in the car than on the trail. However, sometimes shuttling makes sense. There are a few options to do this ride as a loop, but all involve additional climbing or lengthy road rides. As it stands, this ride covers an amazing cross section of the Cleveland National Forest. The climb is substantial but not overwhelming. The second half of the ride runs completely downhill, on fire road and singletrack, dropping 4,400 feet over the course of 11 scenic, stoke-inducing miles. You won't be disappointed.

Crank up Maples Springs Road. The initial paved section follows the creek up Silverado Canyon. After 3 miles the pavement ends and the road climbs above the base of the canyon. Continue pushing uphill—the grade is constant but never steep—following a series of broad zigzags to the Main Divide. Near 6.9 miles continue straight through a white metal gate. Just past the gate, at 7.2 miles, you'll reach Four Corners: the intersection of Maple Springs Road, the Harding Truck Trail, and Main Divide Road.

Turn right on Main Divide Road and keep pushing uphill. The road winds around the perimeter of Modjeska Peak. A carpet of loose rocks makes for tough going in a couple of sections. Don't be discouraged—it gets easier. Near 8.6 miles the climb ends and the road drops modestly to the saddle between Modjeska and Santiago peaks.

At 9.8 miles, just before Main Divide Road turns uphill again, fork left on the Saddle Trail. Get in a low gear and climb hard. The narrow trail follows a steep course through a thick tunnel of manzanita. Be prepared to hike-a-bike. Eventually the Saddle Trail crosses to the Corona (northeast) side of the Santa Ana range and reconnects with Main Divide Road. This is the high point of the ride—5,424 feet—and Santiago Peak looms directly overhead.

At 10.5 miles turn left on Main Divide Road and charge downhill. The road drops quickly down the northeast face of Santiago Peak. Near 11.5 miles a hairpin turn cuts through a wide clearing. This is a popular playground for motorcycle riders (you'll see plenty of tracks). This also marks the beginning of the Upper Holy Jim Trail. If you wish to take this option, turn left between two cairns and head down the technical trail. Be sure to continue straight after 0.3 miles, not turning left on the Coldwater Trail. The Upper Holy Jim Trail switchbacks steeply downhill and reconnects with Main Divide Road.

If you don't wish to ride Upper Holy Jim Trail, stay on Main Divide Road to 13.1 miles. The main section of the Holy Jim Trail begins in a shady grove of pine trees, not far from the bottom of the Upper Holy Jim Trail. Turn right on the Holy Jim Trail. Just past the trail marker is a short steep section, but it only lasts about 20 yards. For the most part, the trail runs smooth and fast. Watch out for hikers, but enjoy. This is pure, unadulterated fun. After leaving the trees, Holy Jim Trail makes a lengthy traverse to the south, then switchbacks down to Holy Jim Canyon. Veer right at 16.6 miles, staying on the main trail. The left option climbs to Holy Jim Falls. The final section of singletrack winds along the tree-lined creek bed. There are several stream crossings, most of which require portaging.

Past 17.5 miles continue straight through a gate. The trail widens to a dirt road and passes by a few cabins. At 18.1 miles turn right on Trabuco Creek Road. Crank out the final miles, all downhill, to the endpoint. The dirt road is bumpy and full of potholes, but it's fast and easy to ride. Look out for cars and trucks along the way: you'll be moving faster, but they're bigger. At 22.5 miles the road ends where your second car is parked. You can look back at Santiago Peak and trace the descent you just made. Hopefully, you didn't leave your keys up there.

After the Ride

If you're heading toward Orange, stop by Johnny Reb's on Chapman Avenue. The kitschy Southern-fried diner is casual enough for even the grittiest of riders. They offer a fine selection of beers on tap, and the fried pickles are amazing (no kidding).

Johnny Reb's
2940 East Chapman Avenue
Orange, CA 92689
(714) 633-3369

GPS TRAILHEAD COORDINATES (WGS 84)	GPS TRAILHEAD COORDINATES (WGS 84)
Starting Points	Ending Points
UTM (WGS84) Zone 11S	UTM Zone (WGS84) 11S
Easting 0445948	Easting 0445699
Northing 3734314	Northing 3724538
Latitude N 33°44'51"	Latitude N 33°39'34"
Longitude W 117°35'01"	Longitude W 117°35'08"

SIERRA PEAK

<table>
<tr><td>

KEY AT-A-GLANCE INFORMATION

</td></tr>
</table>

KEY AT-A-GLANCE INFORMATION

Length: 22 miles

Configuration: Out-and-back

Aerobic difficulty: Moderate to difficult; a lengthy but mostly gradual climb

Technical difficulty: Easy to moderate; all fire road

Exposure: Complete sun except for a few oases of shade

Scenery: Scenic rolling hills in Black Star Canyon, fantastic views from Sierra Peak

Trail traffic: Light to moderate

Riding time: 2.75–4.5 hours

Access: Free parking is available near the trailhead in the dirt shoulders of Black Star Canyon Road.

Special comments: See the note at the end of the ride description for important details about parking.

GPS TRAILHEAD COORDINATES (WGS 84)

UTM Zone (WGS84) 11S
Easting 0437220
Northing 3736226
Latitude N 33°45'51"
Longitude W 117°40'41"

In Brief

Make the long gradual climb up Black Star Canyon to Main Divide Road. Turn left at the divide and ride to Sierra Peak. After a few rolling climbs, you'll be at the signal towers. Enjoy the view and then begin to retrace your route home. Be sure to take the short detour to Beek's Place, near the top of Black Star Canyon Road. You can enjoy the shade and scenery before whipping down the long descent to the trailhead.

Description

For years Black Star Canyon was a troublesome spot for Orange County mountain bikers and hikers. Even though the Silverado Modjeska Recreation and Parks District had an easement for public access along the private sections of Black Star Canyon Road, a few local residents (one in particular) tended to harass the individuals who traveled the road. Those days, apparently, have passed. After law-enforcement officials began enforcing the public right of

DIRECTIONS

From the intersection of the CA 405 freeway and CA 133: Head south on CA405 1.4 miles and exit at Bake Parkway (Exit 1B). Turn left on Bake Parkway, continue 5.3 miles, and turn right on Portola Parkway. After 0.7 miles, turn left on Glenn Ranch Road. Go 1.6 miles and turn left on El Toro Road. After 2 miles, at Cook's Corner, El Toro Road becomes Santiago Canyon Road. Continue another 5.8 miles to Silverado Canyon. Turn right on Silverado Canyon Road and then immediately left on Black Star Canyon Road. Go 1.1 miles on Black Star Canyon Road to the trailhead.

From the intersection of the CA 5 freeway and CA 55: Go north on CA 55 for 3.2 miles and exit at Chapman Avenue. Turn right and then continue straight as Chapman Avenue becomes Santiago Canyon Road. At 9.3 miles from CA 55, turn left on Silverado Canyon Road, and then immediately left on Black Star Canyon Road. Go 1.1 miles on Black Star Canyon Road to the trailhead.

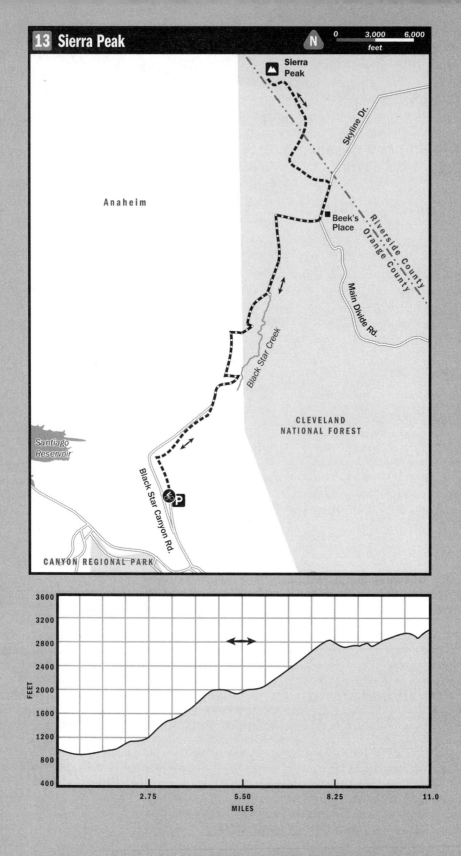

0   3,000   6,000
feet
N

Sierra
Peak

Skyline Dr.

Anaheim

Beek's
Place

Riverside County
Orange County

Main Divide Rd.

Black Star Creek

CLEVELAND
NATIONAL FOREST

Santiago
Reservoir

Black Star Canyon Rd.

P

CANYON REGIONAL PARK

3600
3200
2800
2400
2000
1600
1200
800
400

FEET

2.75   5.50   8.25   11.0
MILES

way, the problems with the residents ceased (You can google "Black Star Canyon" if you want details. There are plenty of stories and anecdotes.) These days Black Star Canyon is more popular than ever. Easy access and free parking (although see the note at the end of this profile) lure plenty of hikers and bikers. Furthermore, unlike Maple Springs Road and the Harding Truck Trail, Black Star Canyon Road is private and therefore inaccessible to most vehicular traffic.

The two most common rides from Black Star Canyon are the out-and-back to Beek's Place and the loop along Main Divide Road to the Silverado Motorway downhill (see Ride 14, page 67), a demanding training ride. Most recreational riders seem to favor the less demanding Beek's Place climb. The extra trip out to Sierra Peak seems a less popular but worthwhile venture. On a clear day you can expect spectacular views from beneath the signal towers. If you've never been to Sierra Peak, and have only seen the signal towers while driving down the CA 91 freeway, you deserve to make at least one trip out there. The good news is that, once you've made the divide, the trip out to Sierra Peak is relatively painless.

Begin at the gate and continue up the pavement on Black Star Canyon Road. After 0.6 miles the road makes a hard right and the pavement ends. Be sure to stay on the main road—there are plenty of NO TRESPASSING signs to remind you.

Near 2.4 miles the road begins to climb in earnest, switchbacking above the bottom of Black Star Canyon. You'll notice a series of homemade speed bumps after the first turn of the climb: keep these in mind; you'll approach the small bumps at speed during your descent. The climb continues steadily for the next 2 miles. The grade isn't brutal, but it will definitely get your heart pumping.

A slight reprieve comes after 4.5 miles, as the road drops into Hidden Ranch. The former cattle ranch, tucked away in a small canyon, is one of the scenic highlights of the ride. There aren't any structures left at the ranch site, but the area is quite scenic, complete with live oak groves, rolling hillsides, and a verdant creek bed. Enjoy the scenery and the short, flat section of road. Past the ranch area, the ascent continues. Crank uphill: you'll see your target, the divide, looming above. Closer to the top, at 7 miles, stay straight and on the main road. At 7.6 miles you'll reach a gate, and at 7.7 miles, Main Divide Road.

Turn left on Main Divide Road and head toward the signal towers and Sierra Peak. The road runs downhill to an intersection with Skyline Drive at 8.2 miles. Continue straight, climbing past a series of extremely tall telephone poles held erect by guy wires. Continue riding along the rolling course to the peak. Several side roads intersect Main Divide Road, but just keep heading toward the signal towers.

One final climb leads to Sierra Peak. Pass through a gate and continue to the top. The slope of the Santa Ana Mountains drops precipitously down from Sierra Peak to the CA 91 freeway corridor. Enjoy the unobstructed views of the Chino Hills, Prado Dam, the San Gabriel Mountains, and most of the Los Angeles basin. Since it tends to be windy at the peak, a light jacket or Windbreaker might be necessary as you relish the scenery and solitude.

The route back is easy and obvious. Crank through the few short climbs along the divide. The only ascent worth mentioning comes between Skyline Drive and Black Star

Black Star Canyon Road coursing through Hidden Ranch

Canyon. Beek's Place is a short but worthwhile detour before you head down Black Star Canyon Road. The old homesite is shady and scenic. You can check out the remnants of the stone structures built by Joseph Beek in the 1930s. Beek, a former Newport Harbor Master who founded the Balboa Island ferry, used the cabin for weekend getaways. Obviously nobody lives at Beek's Place anymore, but on weekends you are bound to encounter other riders and motorists taking a respite under the shade of the conifers that line the property.

The final part of the ride, the return down Black Star Canyon, runs fast and smooth. Cascade down the winding road and then spin out the canyon to the startpoint.

Note: Parking is technically legal on most parts of Black Star Canyon Road. Make sure your car is completely off the road (and on the dirt) and not near any of the posted no parking areas. Some individuals in the notorious Orange County Sheriff Department will ticket *legally* parked cars on Black Star Canyon. You will greatly reduce your chance of receiving an unwarranted citation by parking a few hundred yards away from the trailhead. One section of the road is posted NO PARKING 10 p.m.–3 a.m. This is generally considered a safe place to park during the day, since the absolute directive of the sign doesn't allow for any "gray area" citations.

14

(i) KEY AT-A-GLANCE INFORMATION

Length: 25.7 miles

Configuration: Loop

Aerobic difficulty: Difficult; the first 10-plus miles are nearly all climbing.

Technical difficulty: Moderate

Exposure: Mostly complete sun

Scenery: Pastoral splendor in Black Star Canyon, bird's-eye views from the Main Divide, canyon views from the Silverado Motorway

Trail traffic: Light to moderate; more in the months before the Vision Quest (see Description)

Riding time: 2.75–4.5 hours

Access: Free parking is available near the trailhead on the dirt shoulders of Black Star Canyon Road.

Special comments: See the note at the end of the description of Ride 13 for important details about parking.

GPS TRAILHEAD COORDINATES (WGS 84)

UTM Zone (WGS84) 11S
Easting 0437220
Northing 3736226
Latitude N 33°45'51"
Longitude W 117°40'41"

BLACK STAR CANYON TO MOTORWAY LOOP

In Brief

Push up the long, gradual climb on Black Star Canyon Road. Turn right on Main Divide Road and continue cranking uphill. The steepest climb comes near the 10-mile point as you approach Pleasants Peak. Continue past the peak along the divide, dropping and climbing several more times until you reach the Silverado Motorway. Charge down the length of the rocky singletrack to Silverado Canyon. The ride's last 7 miles are paved and almost entirely downhill. Breeze down Silverado Canyon Road and finish the loop on Black Star Canyon Road.

Description

Since 1997, the Warrior's Society has hosted the Vision Quest, a monumental mountain bike race in the Santa Ana Mountains. The race, now an annual spring event, entails 11,000 feet of climbing over 56.5 grueling miles.

DIRECTIONS

From the intersection of the CA 405 freeway and the CA 133 freeway: Head south on CA 405 1.4 miles and exit at Bake Parkway (Exit 1B). Turn left on Bake Parkway, continue 5.3 miles, and turn right on Portola Parkway. After 0.7 miles, turn left on Glenn Ranch Road. Go 1.6 miles and turn left on El Toro Road. After 2 miles, at Cook's Corner, El Toro Road becomes Santiago Canyon Road. Continue another 5.8 miles to Silverado Canyon. Turn right on Silverado Canyon Road and then immediately left on Black Star Canyon Road. Go 1.1 miles on Black Star Canyon Road to the trailhead.

From the intersection of the CA 5 and CA 66 freeways: Go north on CA 55 for 3.2 miles and exit at Chapman Avenue. Turn right and then continue straight as Chapman Avenue becomes Santiago Canyon Road. At 9.3 miles from CA 55, turn left on Silverado Canyon, and then immediately left on Black Star Canyon Road. Go 1.1 miles on Black Star Canyon Road to the trailhead.

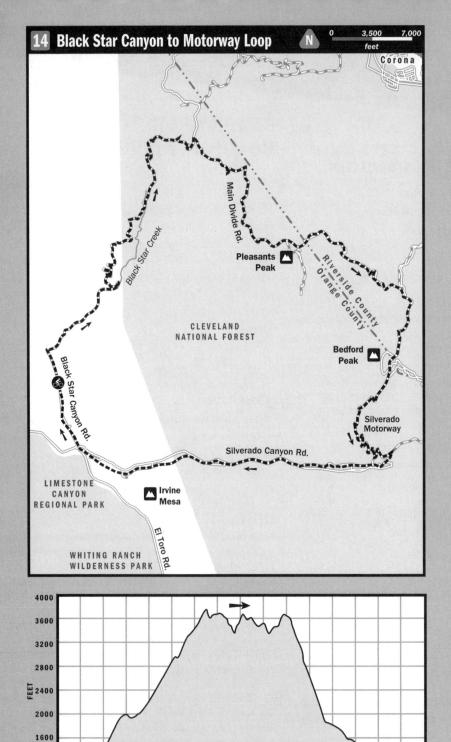

The first leg of the Vision Quest begins at the base of Black Star Canyon Road and ends at the bottom of the Silverado Motorway. The course continues up Maple Springs Road to the Main Divide, then descends down the Holy Jim Trail, goes up West Horsethief Trail, down the Trabuco Trail, and finishes on Trabuco Creek Road. In 1997, only a few committed riders completed the course. However, now capped at 110 participants, the Vision Quest has sold out the last few years. There is also a shorter, 42-mile, version of the race known as the Counting Coup. Both races are run simultaneously. (Check the Warrior's Society Web site, **www.warriorssociety.org**, for dates and information.)

In the weeks before the Vision Quest, this loop, covering the first stage of the race, is popular with riders training for the event. Whether or not you intend to attempt the Vision Quest, the Black Star Canyon to Motorway Loop is a great training ride—4,600 feet of climbing, a long downhill to keep your skills sharp, and 7 miles of road riding to cool down on.

Hoist your bike over a gate and begin riding up Black Star Canyon Road. The road runs fairly level for the first 2-plus miles. You'll pass by several private lots with posted NO TRESPASSING signs. Heed the signs and stay on the road: Black Star residents are notoriously testy about their property rights.

The road hairpins after 2.4 miles and begins to ascend above the canyon. Crank hard through 2 miles of climbing switchbacks. At 4.5 miles make the short, gradual drop to the Hidden Ranch area. You'll cross a couple of cattle guards, although the cattle are long gone. This is private land, but a public-parks easement allows for legal passage via the dirt road. However, you must stay on the road.

Climb past Hidden Ranch. You'll gain elevation quickly, allowing for great views. Stay to the right at 7 miles, following the main road. You'll pass through a gate near 7.6 miles and reach Main Divide Road at 7.7 miles. Turn right on Main Divide Road and continue climbing—the next couple of miles are the most difficult of the ride. Just keep your mindset—climb, climb, climb. The road finally tops out after 10.2 miles. A short drop is followed by another short ascent. You'll pass the turnoff for Pleasants Peak near 11 miles: stay left and on the divide, unless you feel the need for extra climbing.

The next few miles follow the undulating divide. Keep as much momentum as possible from the downhill sections to help with the ascents. Unfortunately, many of the climbs are steep and some follow sharp, speed-negating, turns. The good news is that the views are gorgeous. Try to enjoy the scenery and forget about the hard work.

Finally, at 15.5 miles, you'll reach Bedford Peak and the top of the Silverado Motorway. Step over a low wooden barrier and head down the trail. Stay left as the Silverado Motorway follows a rounded ridge. The trail quickly narrows, traversing a rocky hillside. Fork left at 16.5 miles and rip down the switchbacks toward Silverado Canyon. There are plenty of small rocks but few other surprises on the trail. Let your suspension do the work and enjoy.

You'll reach Maple Springs Road near 18.6 miles. Turn right and head down the paved road. After a stream crossing, pass through a gate onto Silverado Canyon Road, which runs gently downhill. The road is narrow, but push a big gear and you'll be able to ride at the same speed as the cars. Near 24.2 miles you'll see the turnoff for Black Star Canyon Road. Turn right and cruise the final bit of road to complete the loop.

15

THE JOPLIN TRAIL

KEY AT-A-GLANCE INFORMATION

Length: 23.4 miles

Configuration: Loop

Aerobic difficulty: Difficult; a long climb to the divide is followed by a taxing descent. Several short climbs and drops finish the ride.

Technical difficulty: Difficult; the descent on the Joplin Trail courses over loose, rocky terrain. Expect plenty of obstacles and challenging sections on the narrow trail.

Exposure: Mostly complete sun

Scenery: Panoramic and unobstructed views from the Harding Truck Trail and the Main Divide. Riparian foliage completely encloses most of the Joplin Trail.

Trail traffic: Light

Riding time: 3–5 hours

Access: Free parking is available at the bottom of the Harding Truck Trail. The parking is provided by the Tucker Wildlife Center, so consider giving a small donation to the center for use of their space. If there are no spaces at Tucker, parking is also available near the route on the Modjeska Grade, just downhill from the beginning of the Santiago Truck Trail.

GPS TRAILHEAD COORDINATES (WGS 84)

UTM Zone (WGS84)   11S
Easting   0442682
Northing   3730236
Latitude   N 33°42'38"
Longitude   W 117°37'07"

In Brief

There is nothing brief about this ride. Crank 8.9 miles to the top of the Harding Truck Trail. Turn right on Main Divide Road and continue climbing. You'll ride around (but not up to) Modjeska Peak. The Joplin Trail drops from the saddle between Modjeska and Santiago peaks. Turn right on Joplin and make the harrowing, hairball descent to Old Camp—2 miles of challenging trail riding that will not disappoint. From Old Camp, push up the short climb up the ridge and the start of the Santiago Truck Trail. Then charge down the Santiago Truck ridgeline trail—it's mostly singletrack with short sections of fire road—to the gate at the Modjeska Grade. Turn right on pavement and coast downhill to Modjeska Canyon Road. A short ride up the narrow canyon completes the loop.

Description

The Joplin Trail is one of the great trails of Orange County. This precipice disguised as a singletrack drops from the

DIRECTIONS

From the intersection of the CA 405 and CA 133 freeways: Head south on CA 405 1.4 miles and exit at Bake Parkway (Exit 1B). Turn left on Bake Parkway, continue 5.3 miles, and turn right on Portola Parkway. After 0.7 miles, turn left on Glenn Ranch Road. Go 1.6 miles and turn left on El Toro Road. After 2 miles, at Cook's Corner, El Toro Road becomes Santiago Canyon Road. Continue another 1.3 miles and turn right on the Modjeska Grade. Follow the grade over the hill to Modjeska Canyon Road. Turn right and go 1.2 miles to the Tucker Wildlife Sanctuary.

From the intersection of the CA 5 and CA 55 freeways: Go north on CA 55 for 3.2 miles and exit at Chapman Avenue. Turn right and then continue straight as Chapman Avenue becomes Santiago Canyon Road. At 13.5 miles from CA 55, turn left on Modjeska Canyon Road. After 0.9 miles, at an intersection with the Modjeska Grade, stay left on Modjeska Canyon Road and continue another 1.2 miles to the Tucker Wildlife Sanctuary.

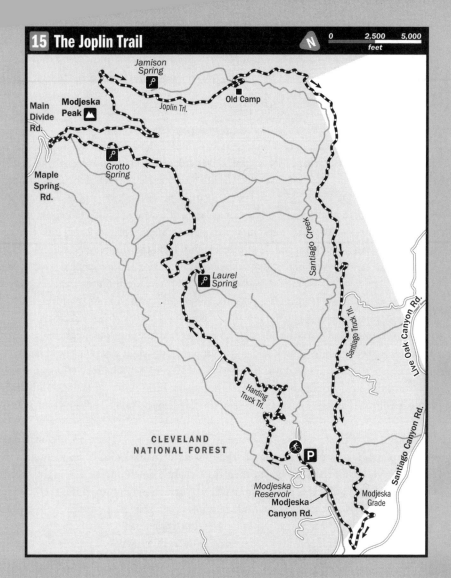

0   2,500   5,000
feet

Jamison
Spring

Main
Divide
Rd.

Modjeska
Peak

Joplin Trl.

Old Camp

Grotto
Spring

Maple
Spring
Rd.

Laurel
Spring

Santiago Creek

Santiago Truck Trl.

Live Oak Canyon Rd.

CLEVELAND
NATIONAL FOREST

Harding
Truck Trl.

P

Modjeska
Reservoir
Modjeska
Canyon Rd.

Modjeska
Grade

Santiago Canyon Rd.

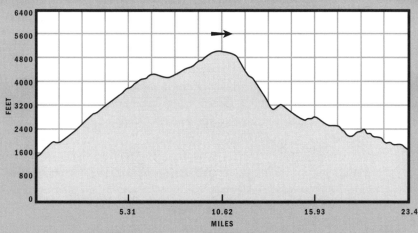

FEET				
6400				
5600				
4800				
4000				
3200				
2400				
1600				
800				
0	5.31	10.62	15.93	23.4

MILES

saddle between Modjeska and Santiago peaks to a remote fire pit in the trees known as Old Camp. Joplin rivals both the Trabuco Trail and the San Juan Trail for scenic splendor and is much more technically challenging and remote than either of those. The remoteness is what makes Joplin special. Since the trail is difficult to reach, and a car shuttle almost impossible to arrange, traffic on the trail is generally sparse.

This loop, which includes a long grind up the Harding Truck Trail and a somewhat taxing return on the Santiago Truck Trail, is difficult and time consuming. If you don't feel entirely up to the task, a few shorter options are described at the end of the Description.

The ride up the Harding Truck Trail is nearly 2 miles longer than the climb up Maple Springs Road (both roads ascend to the same place on the Main Divide). Moreover, the climb up Harding is generally steeper and more taxing than Maple Springs Road. This is because the Harding Truck Trail has two downhill sections amid the climbing (shedding elevation means more overall climbing) and a surface that is rockier and looser than that of Maple Springs Road. If you can climb Maple Springs Road in 80–90 minutes, expect to take two full hours climbing the Harding Truck Trail. The advantage of climbing Harding is that you don't have to compete with vehicular traffic—closed gates prevent vehicle access.

The Harding Truck Trail road starts steep. Get in a low gear, push past the gate across from the Tucker Wildlife Center, and start climbing. Stay right where the road forks at 0.4 miles—the left option drops down to the Modjeska Reservoir. The road climbs for about 1 mile, then descends briefly as it crosses a tight canyon. Keep climbing; soon you will be high above Modjeska Canyon, taking in views of the Saddleback Valley and the Orange County coast.

Near 4.8 miles you will pass the turnoff to Laurel Springs. There are unsubstantiated rumors of drinking water here, but the trail is overgrown and probably best left alone. Past 6.6 miles the road finally levels and then runs slightly downhill. It's a straight shot on a smooth surface, so you can pedal hard and carry some momentum to the final climb. At 8.8 miles you will reach a gate; continue straight here. Turn momentarily right on Maple Springs Road and right again, at 9 miles, on Main Divide Road.

Head south on Main Divide Road, climbing the rock-strewn road around the south face of Modjeska Peak. Near 10.3 miles you will reach the high point of the ride at 5,027 feet. This is a good place to take a break, enjoy the incredible view, and have a bite to eat. You'll be able to see bottom of the Joplin Trail, 2,000 feet below. Trees and the sharp contours of the hillside obscure the remainder of the trail.

Main Divide Road drops slightly as it heads toward Santiago Peak. The Joplin Trail begins near 11.4 miles, just before the road crosses the saddle and resumes climbing. Lower your seat and turn right on singletrack. It's only 2 miles to Old Camp, but it feels much longer . . . and that's a good thing. Course across loose hillsides, over rocks and ledges, down rutty drops, through off-camber turns, and amid logs and water. This trail has every obstacle imaginable, and most of them are challenging. There are a couple of short climbs on the trail, but they are hardly worth mentioning. Your mind-set should be all downhill.

At 13.7 miles you will reach Old Camp. Today, the place is just a fire pit set under a quiet canopy of trees. But various legends say it was an old Native American camp, a temporary home for fugitives, or an old miner's camp. In fact, it was actually a California Conservation Corps camp. Turn left at the fire pit and climb up the rocky trail to the ridgeline. At 14.2 miles a clearing marks the beginning of the Santiago Truck Trail (this first section is sometimes called the Upper Santiago Trail). Head downhill along the ridge on the fast, fun singletrack. At 15.5 miles veer right at a fork and stay on the ridge—the left fork drops to Trabuco Creek Road. The trail continues downhill, even switchbacking at one point. Near 18.2 miles you will see two flags masted on a small hill. These mark the beginning of The Luge (see Ride 9, page 50). Continue straight and muster your last remaining energy to climb another rocky slope. The trail alternates between singletrack and dirt road as it courses along the ridge. After two more short climbs—and a lot of downhill—you will reach the Modjeska Grade at 21.5 miles. Go through the gate and turn right on pavement. Coast down the winding road to Modjeska Canyon. Turn right, up Modjeska Canyon Road, at 22.4 miles, and spin out the last mile to complete the loop.

There are shuttle options to this ride. A somewhat less taxing and fun route would be to begin on Maple Springs Road and end at Cook's Corner via a drop down The Luge. You could also descend the unnamed road from the Upper Santiago Trail to the bottom of Trabuco Creek Road (this is, perhaps, less desirable than the first option). Both of these alternative routes will involve extra driving time and the need for a second car, but will save your legs a bit of climbing.

Note about other parking options: Farther from the trailhead, there is some parking on Santiago Canyon Road and, even farther, in the dirt lot near Cook's Corner (this option only really works if you are doing a shuttle ride). You may also find spots on Modjeska Canyon Road, but inquire with a local resident before you park your vehicle.

After the Ride

Once again Cook's Corner is probably your best bet. On weekend afternoons the roadhouse will be overrun with Harley riders, but the beer is good, the pool tables nearly level, and the food adequately filling.

Cook's Corner
19122 Live Oak Canyon Road
Trabuco Canyon, CA 92679
(949) 858-0266

16

KEY AT-A-GLANCE INFORMATION

Length: 17.2 miles

Configuration: Loop

Aerobic difficulty: Difficult; one big climb, then several more climbs

Technical difficulty: Moderate to difficult; the Trabuco Trail may be the best downhill around, but it does have some rocky sections

Exposure: Varied; full sun for most of the Main Divide traverse

Scenery: Pristine wilderness with stunning views; you won't believe you're in Orange County.

Trail traffic: Light to moderate; lower parts of Holy Jim and Trabuco trails are crowded on weekends.

Riding time: 2.5–4 hours

Access: In the Cleveland National Forest. Park in lot near the Holy Jim trailhead. If full, park near the Holy Jim fire station or on any spur off Trabuco Creek Road. $5 day-use fee for national forest. If you don't have an Adventure Pass, use payment envelopes available at base of Holy Jim Trail. Purchase daily or annual Adventure Passes on the U.S. Forest Service Web site or at local sporting-goods stores such as Sportmart, Big 5, and Sport Chalet.

GPS TRAILHEAD COORDINATES (WGS 84)

UTM Zone (WGS84)   11S
Easting   0452060
Northing   3726468
Latitude   N 33°40'37"
Longitude   W 117°31'02"

In Brief

Make the long climb up Holy Jim Trail. The trail begins in a stream-fed canyon, then switchbacks up toward Santiago Peak. Before you reach the peak, turn right on Main Divide Road. It's a long, arduous trek along the divide to the top of Trabuco Trail. You'll make several more climbs, including a steep, grueling ascent just past the turnoff to Indian Truck Trail. When you reach Trabuco Trail, you'll be more than ready to head downhill. Luckily, it's a great trail, one of the best around. Charge down the length of the Trabuco Trail and then follow Trabuco Creek Road back to the trailhead.

Description

In its initial stages the Holy Jim Trail makes several crossings through a rock-strewn streambed; unless you are a highly skilled trials rider, expect to carry your bike over the stream crossings. Past the turnoff to Holy Jim Falls, at 1.4 miles, the trail begins to ascend in earnest, switchbacking

DIRECTIONS

From the intersection of the CA 405 freeway and the CA 133 freeway: Head south on CA 405 1.4 miles and exit at Bake Parkway (Exit 1B). Turn left on Bake Parkway, go 5.3 miles, and turn right on Portola Parkway. After 0.7 miles turn left on Glenn Ranch Road. Go 1.6 miles and turn left on El Toro Road. After 2 miles, at Cook's Corner, El Toro becomes Santiago Canyon Road. Here turn right on Live Oak Canyon and go 4.3 miles to Trabuco Creek Road. Turn left on Trabuco Creek Road and follow the dirt road 4.5 miles to the trailhead. (Expect the drive up Trabuco Creek Road to take 20–30 minutes.)

From the intersection of the CA 5 and CA 66 freeways: Go north on CA 55 3.2 miles and exit at Chapman Avenue. Turn right on Chapman Avenue and continue straight as Chapman Avenue becomes Santiago Canyon Road. At 15.1 miles from CA 55, you'll see Cook's Corner on the left. Turn left on Live Oak Canyon Road and go 4.3 miles to Trabuco Creek Road. Turn left on Trabuco Creek Road and follow the dirt road 4.5 miles to the trailhead. (Expect the drive up Trabuco Creek Road to take 20–30 minutes.)

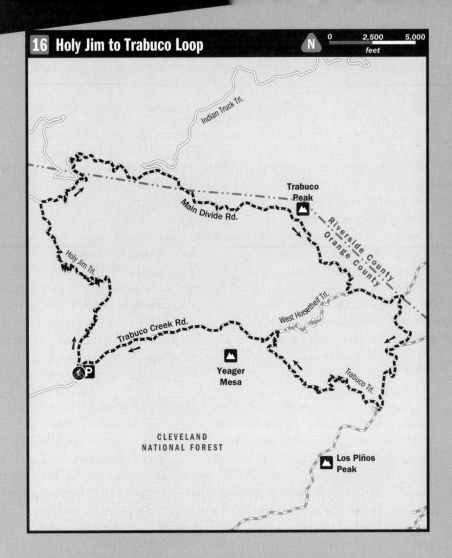

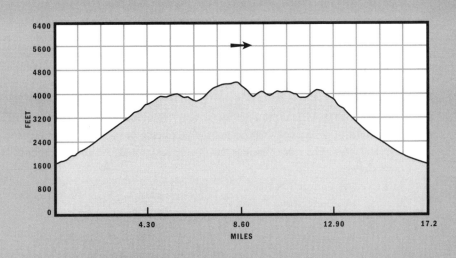

up a brush-lined hillside. Many of the switchbacks are tight, but when you get in a groove, you'll find yourself cleaning one after another—just keep your weight forward and maintain momentum through each turn.

Past the switchbacks, crank the final, tree-lined section of Holy Jim Trail up to Main Divide Road. (From here, Upper Holy Jim Trail continues to Santiago Peak, but it's a natty trail that is best ridden downhill.) Turn right on Main Divide Road and, whatever you do, don't tell your fellow riders (or yourself) that the climbing is over. It seems every traverse along the Main Divide involves more climbing than expected, and this ride is no exception. Half of this route's 4,500 feet of total climbing occurs along the Main Divide.

Initially, from the Holy Jim Trail, the road runs downhill, coursing through a stand of trees on an east-facing slope. *Remember:* Main Divide Road is open to vehicular traffic. Generally the drivers and motorcyclists are cautious and respectful, and you should be as well. Be careful around blind turns and stay to the right of the road when possible.

Near 6.4 miles you'll pass the turnoff for the Indian Truck Trail, but don't take it unless you want to go to Corona. Stay straight and push up a long, steep ascent. This is the longest and most difficult climb on the divide, but it isn't the last of this route. The road continues along the spine of the Santa Ana Mountains, winding, dipping, and climbing. The downhill sections go by quickly, and the climbs just keep coming. You'll reach the turnoff for the West Horsethief Trail at 9.6 miles. You could bail out here and head straight down, but you might as well keep going.

After two more climbs, at 12.1 miles, you'll reach the top of the Trabuco Trail. Rejoice. It's all downhill from here. As of this writing, the Trabuco Trail is in excellent condition. A fantastic downhill, it may trump the San Juan Trail as the best singletrack in Orange County. The top of the trail is fast and smooth, winding through trees and massive collections of manzanita. There are plenty of blind turns, so be mindful of other bikers and also hikers. The trail becomes progressively rockier as it winds down toward Trabuco Creek. There are no extreme challenges or drop-offs, just a series of fun, moderately technical sections. You'll pass the West Horsethief Trail at 14.6 miles, but continue on the Trabuco Trail, keeping momentum and bouncing over the rocks. The trail ends at 16.3 miles. Continue through a gate and then go straight on Trabuco Creek Road. Cruise downhill on the dirt road to complete the loop.

Note: The Holy Jim Trail is near the end of Trabuco Creek Road. If your car is not dirt-road worthy, consider beginning the ride at the intersection of Trabuco Creek and Live Oak Canyon roads, which adds an additional 9 miles of peddling. Trabuco Creek Road is private, so drive slowly and respect the local residents. There is a chance of poison-oak exposure on this ride. Take the necessary precautions.

After the Ride

Bring beer and food in a cooler: you deserve it, and will probably need it, after this ride. If that isn't enough, stop by Cook's Corner on the way home (it takes 30–40 minutes to get there from Holy Jim). The roadhouse has lots of beer on tap and serviceable bar food.

Cook's Corner
19122 Live Oak Canyon Road
Trabuco Canyon, CA 92679
(949) 858-0266

17

WEST HORSETHIEF

KEY AT-A-GLANCE INFORMATION

Length: 8.5 miles

Configuration: Out-and-back

Aerobic difficulty: Moderate to difficult, depending on how much of the climb you can ride

Technical difficulty: Difficult; no steep sections or drop-offs, but plenty of rocks and a few narrow cliff-side traverses

Exposure: Plentiful shade in the canyon but full sun on the climb

Scenery: Pristine wilderness; lush flora in the canyon and stunning views from the Main Divide

Trail traffic: Light

Riding time: 1.75–2.5 hours or more

Access: The entire ride is in the Cleveland National Forest. Park in lot near the Holy Jim trailhead. If full, park near the Holy Jim fire station or on any spur off of Trabuco Creek Road. $5 day-use fee for the national forest. If you don't have an Adventure Pass, use the payment envelopes available at base of the Holy Jim Trail. Purchase daily or annual Adventure Passes on the U.S. Forest Service Web site or at local sporting-goods stores such as Sportmart, Big 5, and Sport Chalet.

GPS TRAILHEAD COORDINATES (WGS 84)

UTM Zone (WGS84) 11S
Easting 0452060
Northing 3726468
Latitude N 33°40'37"
Longitude W 117°31'02"

In Brief

Don't be fooled by the relatively short length. This ride covers remote and somewhat demanding terrain. Begin at the Holy Jim trailhead and crank up Trabuco Creek Road. In less than a mile the road ends and the Trabuco Trail begins. Continue up the canyon on the singletrack—it's not steep, but the rocky terrain offers a worthy challenge. Turn left on the West Horsethief Trail and climb to the top. Expect to walk some, if not all, of the climb—it's steep. Enjoy the view at the Main Divide, then turn around and head back downhill. The return route is fast and fun. It's amazing what you can do when gravity is on your side.

Description

After driving all the way to Holy Jim, you'll be happy to get out of the car and start riding. The canyon road climbs

DIRECTIONS

From the intersection of the CA 405 and CA 133 freeways: Head south on CA 405 1.4 miles and exit at Bake Parkway (Exit 1B). Turn left on Bake Parkway, go 5.3 miles, and turn right on Portola Parkway. After 0.7 miles turn left on Glenn Ranch Road. Go 1.6 miles and turn left on El Toro Road. After 2 miles, at Cook's Corner, El Toro becomes Santiago Canyon Road. Here turn right on Live Oak Canyon Road and go 4.3 miles to Trabuco Creek Road. Turn left on Trabuco Creek Road and follow the dirt road 4.5 miles to the trailhead. (Expect the drive up Trabuco Creek Road to take 20–30 minutes.)

From the intersection of the CA 5 and CA 55 freeways: Go north on CA 55 3.2 miles and exit at Chapman Avenue. Turn right on Chapman Avenue and continue straight as Chapman Avenue becomes Santiago Canyon Road. At 15.1 miles from CA 55, you'll see Cook's Corner on the left. Turn left on Live Oak Canyon Road and go 4.3 miles to Trabuco Creek Road. Turn left on Trabuco Creek Road and follow the dirt road 4.5 miles to the trailhead. (Expect the drive up Trabuco Creek Road to take 20–30 minutes.)

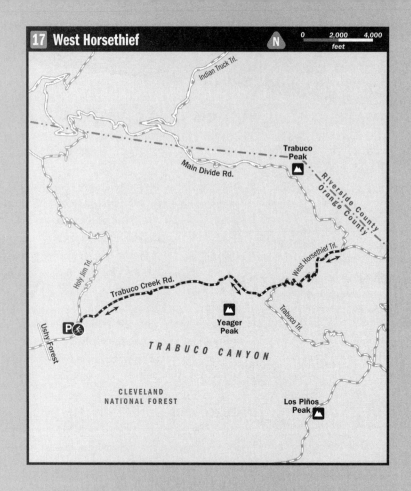

Indian Truck Trl.

Trabuco Peak

Main Divide Rd.

Riverside County
Orange County

West Horsethief Trl.

Holy Jim Trl.

Trabuco Creek Rd.

Ushy Forest

P

Yeager Peak

Trabuco Trl.

T R A B U C O   C A N Y O N

CLEVELAND
NATIONAL FOREST

Los Piños Peak

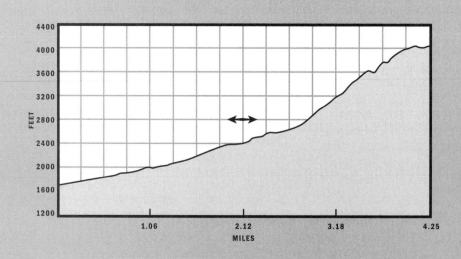

modestly for about 1 more mile. At road's end, go through a gate and onto the Trabuco Trail. The terrain is fairly demanding and should prove challenging for committed riders. Novice riders may find themselves frequently mounting, dismounting, and portaging their bikes.

Follow the creekside singletrack, winding up the canyon, crossing side streams and coursing over rocky escarpments. At points the foliage drapes over the trail and may impede your progress. There is plenty of poison oak in the canyon, so take the proper precautions.

Past 2.4 miles the trail climbs to a T-intersection. Turn left and stay on the Trabuco Trail (the trail to the right is unmaintained and unrideable). At 2.7 miles turn left on the West Horsethief Trail. The Trabuco Trail continues to the right, following a longer course to the Main Divide. The West Horsethief Trail is a shorter route—you'll see its switchbacks cut into the hillside above you. Get ready to climb.

The West Horsethief Trail begins in a narrow canyon. There is a massive collection of ladybugs near the start of the trail. Be prepared to take a few of the critters along for a while. The switchbacks start after 2.8 miles. The trail is steep, narrow, and rocky. Expect to push your bike up some, if not all, of the trail.

The stunning views of Trabuco Canyon should take your mind off the climb. Just keep pushing—and riding when you can. Near 3.9 miles the trail levels somewhat. The rest of the trail ahead is rideable. Just past 4.2 miles you'll reach Main Divide Road. Santiago Peak, the top of the Holy Jim Trail and the highest point in the range, is a couple of miles to the west. Clear days should afford views of much of the Orange County basin, the coast, and beyond.

There are options for the return route: riding to and descending the Holy Jim Trail adds about 10 miles to the loop and plenty more climbing; following the Main Divide to the top of the Trabuco Creek Trail and then heading down adds about 4 miles of riding. The most direct route is obvious . . . and fun. Charge back down the West Horsethief Trail's switchbacks. After the climb you should have intimate knowledge of the trail's topography. Near the bottom one of the switchbacks is narrow and gravel strewn. Watch your speed and stay on the trail. "Don't go over the cliff" is a good mantra: remember it.

Before 6 miles turn right onto the Trabuco Trail. The ride down the canyon is a hoot. You'll bounce over the rocks you struggled over on the way up. Keep your momentum and you'll easily clean the entire trail. Near 7.6 miles the trail gives way to fire road. The rest of the ride is a breeze—all downhill on the dirt road.

Note: Access the trailhead is via Trabuco Creek Road, a private dirt road that begins at Live Oak Canyon Road. Be courteous to the local homeowners: drive slowly to avoid stirring up dust. Past the national-forest boundary, the canyon narrows and the road crosses the creek twice. If you want to ride more and drive less, you may park at any spur along the road, but you will need an Adventure Pass. The only nearby payment kiosk is near the Holy Jim trailhead. If you begin the ride at the intersection of Trabuco Creek and Live Oak Canyon (no fee required), it will mean an additional 9 miles of peddling.

After the Ride

Think ahead and bring food with you. It's roughly a 40-minute drive to the Cook's Corner roadhouse. You might as well hang out near the trailhead and enjoy the scenery.

IRVINE RANCH

18

KEY AT-A-GLANCE INFORMATION

Length: 10.39 miles

Configuration: Loop

Aerobic difficulty: Moderate-plus; nearly all the climbing comes in the first 4 miles

Technical difficulty: Moderate; the singletrack on Limestone Ridge has some fun sections

Exposure: Mostly complete sun

Scenery: Rolling hillsides, oak-lined arroyos, and a stunning geological formation known as The Sinks

Trail traffic: Light; open only to docent groups organized by the Irvine Ranch Land Reserve (IRLR)

Riding time: 1.5–2.5 hours; the Irvine Ranch Land Reserve Web site says the ride will take 3 hours, but most groups will probably finish faster.

Access: Loma Ridge and Limestone Canyon are part of the Irvine Ranch Land Reserve. The land is open to the public, but only via docent-led activities. Docent-led mountain bike rides are generally held every weekend at one of several locations in the reserve.

GPS TRAILHEAD COORDINATES (WGS 84)

UTM Zone (WGS84) 11S
Easting 0435063
Northing 3735486
Latitude N 33°45'27"
Longitude W 117°42'04"

In Brief

Ride out the Irvine Haul Road and then attack the intervals on Loma Ridge—steep, steeper, and steepest. The hard work is finished after 4 miles, so drop down to Bolero Springs and then follow Limestone Canyon to The Sinks. A quick climb up Cactus Canyon takes you to Limestone Ridge. Ride the length of the ridge, eventually dropping back down to Limestone Canyon. A short jaunt on a fire road completes the loop.

Information

www.irvineranchlandreserve.org
(714) 508-4757

To sign up for one of the rides, go to the IRLR Web site, click on "Let's Go Outside," and then scroll down to "Activities." Search under the heading "Programs and Description" for mountain bike rides among the various types of events and activities. This particular ride is

DIRECTIONS

From the intersection of the CA 405 and CA 133 freeways: Head south on CA 405 1.4 miles and exit at Bake Parkway (Exit 1B). Turn left on Bake Parkway, go 5.3 miles, and turn right on Portola Parkway. After 0.7 miles turn left on Glenn Ranch Road. Go 1.6 miles and turn left on El Toro Road. After 2 miles, at Cook's Corner, El Toro becomes Santiago Canyon Road. Continue another 7.7 miles on Santiago Canyon Road. Turn left on a dirt road and head through a gate, where a small sign reads IRVINE RANCH LAND RESERVE: STAGING AREA 1. Continue 100 feet on the dirt road and turn right into the Augustine Staging Area.

From the intersection of the CA 5 and CA 55 freeways: Go north on CA 55 3.2 miles and exit at Chapman Avenue. Turn right and continue straight as Chapman Avenue becomes Santiago Canyon Road. At 7.5 miles from CA 55, turn right on a dirt road and head through a gate, where a small sign reads IRVINE RANCH LAND RESERVE: STAGING AREA 1. Continue 100 feet on the dirt road and turn right into the Augustine Staging Area.

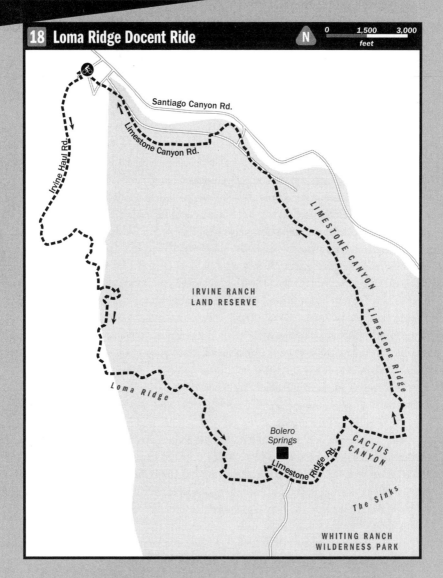

N

0   1,500   3,000
feet

Santiago Canyon Rd.

Limestone Canyon Rd.

Irvine Haul Rd.

IRVINE RANCH
LAND RESERVE

LIMESTONE CANYON

Limestone Ridge

Loma Ridge

Bolero
Springs

CACTUS
CANYON

Limestone Ridge Rd.

The Sinks

WHITING RANCH
WILDERNESS PARK

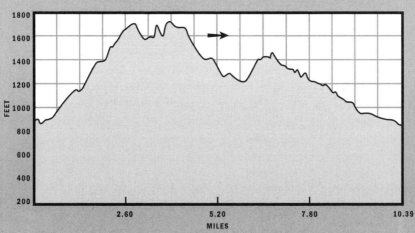

called Loma Ridge to Bolero Springs; it begins at the Augustine Staging Area near Santiago Canyon. The ride is limited to 21 or fewer individuals and it will fill up, so sign up early. The ride leaves promptly at the stated time. Be sure to arrive early, allowing ample time to gear up and ready your bike.

Description

In 2006, in a highly publicized event, local land baron Donald Bren and former Terminator Arnold Schwarzenegger toured some of Orange County's most pristine open space. Yes, they banded together in the name of—stop the presses please!—wilderness preservation. The tour, just two friends on a hike with a gaggle of reporters, did not herald the opening of new parkland. Instead, the media show was designed to promote the newly consolidated map of the Irvine Company's preservation efforts. The Irvine Ranch Land Reserve is now the centerpiece of those efforts.

No matter what you think of the Irvine Company, the quantity and quality of preserved land in the IRLR is magnificent. (The land reserve makes up 50 percent of the ranch's 93,000 acres, according to the IRLR Web site). Some of this land includes accessible (open to the public) riding and hiking areas such as the Laguna Wilderness. Other parcels are accessible only via docent-led tours, most notably Limestone Canyon, Bommer Canyon, and Fremont Canyon. Luckily the IRLR folks offer docent-led mountain bike tours. These are fun, challenging rides, with friendly and knowledgeable guides, covering some of the most pristine and gorgeous scenery in the county. So check out the Web site and don't be discouraged about riding with a group.

This ride begins and ends at the Augustine Staging Area. Ride up the moderate, paved grade of the Irvine Haul Road to Loma Ridge. The fun begins near 1.2 miles. Climb Loma Ridge, a dirt road-cum-doubletrack, ascending sharply to the ridgeline. After just 2.8 miles you'll be close to the high point (in elevation, that is) of the ride. But the climbing is not quite over—make a short drop and then crank up two more intervals. The final climb is known as The Wall; it's steep but thankfully short.

Near 4 miles the road starts downhill. An unremarkable but enjoyable singletrack leads to Bolero Springs. Continue downhill to Limestone Ridge Road and then climb gradually to The Sinks. The view of The Sinks is worth the trip alone. The unusual formation of cliffs and gullies is sometimes called the Grand Canyon of Orange County (but the Grand Canyon, as far as anyone knows, is never referred to as The Sinks of Arizona). Take your picture near the rim and tell all your friends you were there.

Continue through Limestone Canyon, then turn up Cactus Canyon. Cruise beneath a canopy of live oaks and then push up a quick ascent to Limestone Ridge. Turn left on the dirt road, at 6.4 miles, and then, at 6.6 miles, fork left on a fence-line trail. Rip down the narrow ridgeline. The fast and fun singletrack follows an undulating course just above Santiago Canyon. Expect great views of the Santa Ana Mountains and Blackstar Canyon, if you have time to look.

At the end of the singletrack, drop down from the ridge back to Limestone Canyon Road. Spin down the dirt road back to the Augustine Staging Area to complete the loop.

WHITING RANCH

19

WHITING RANCH LOOP

KEY AT-A-GLANCE INFORMATION

Length: 6.29 miles

Configuration: Loop

Aerobic difficulty: Relatively easy

Technical difficulty: Moderate; the Cactus Hill Trail requires decent bike-handling skills.

Exposure: More shade than sun

Scenery: Oak woodland canyons, rolling hills, and craggy hillsides of coastal sage scrub and chaparral

Trail traffic: Moderate to heavy; the park is small and busy.

Riding time: 45 minutes–1.5 hours

Access: The ride begins and ends at the Portola Parkway entrance to Whiting Ranch Regional Park. Parking in the official lot, at Portola and Market, costs $3. Most of the mountain bike community tends to park across the street in the shopping center near Outback Steakhouse. The park is open 7 days a week, 7 a.m.–sunset. Trails may be closed for up to 3 days after any significant rainfall.

Special comments: For a longer ride (approximately 14 miles), connect this loop with The Luge Loop. See the ride description for details.

GPS TRAILHEAD COORDINATES (WGS 84)

UTM Zone (WGS84)   11S

Easting   0438226

Northing   3727068

Latitude   N 33°40'54"

Longitude   W 117°39'59"

In Brief

Crank up the Borrego Trail, a one-way singletrack that darts along a shady creek bed. Turn right on Mustard Road and climb to the ridge at Four Corners. Head south, briefly, on Whiting Road, and then make a sharp left onto the Cactus Hill Trail. Drop down the cactus-lined singletrack to a chaparral-filled canyon. A short, steep climb up the Sage Scrub Trail is followed by another winding descent to Whiting Road. Head down the dirt road for a spell and then cut through the trees on the Serrano Cow Trail to Serrano Road. Serrano Road ends at Portola Parkway. Turn right on the pavement and follow the road back to the trailhead.

Information

Whiting Ranch Regional Park
26695 Portola Parkway
Foothill Ranch, CA 92610
(949) 923-2245

Description

After El Morro, Whiting Ranch Regional Park may be the most popular mountain bike destination in Orange County. It is a small park, a horseshoe of open space surrounded by suburban sprawl, but it contains a surprising number of fun trails. There are two main entrances to Whiting Ranch, one on Portola Parkway and the other on Glenn Ranch Road. From Portola Parkway, the Borrego Trail is a one-way trail for bicyclists (you may only ride

DIRECTIONS

From the Interstate 5 and CA 55 interchange: Take I-5 south 9 miles and exit at Bake Parkway/Lake Forest Drive. Turn left and go 5.3 miles on Bake Parkway, then turn left on Portola Parkway. After 0.2 miles turn left on Market Drive. The trailhead is on the west side of Outback Steakhouse, near the creek.

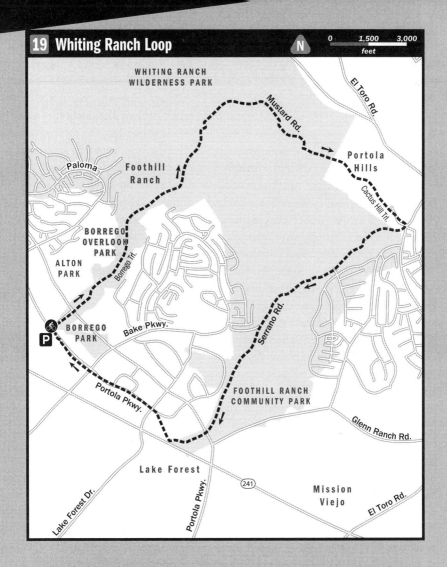

N

0   1,500   3,000
feet

WHITING RANCH
WILDERNESS PARK

El Toro Rd.

Mustard Rd.

Paloma

Foothill
Ranch

Portola
Hills

Cactus Hill Trl.

BORREGO
OVERLOOK
PARK

ALTON
PARK

Borrego Trl.

BORREGO
PARK

Bake Pkwy.

Serrano Rd.

FOOTHILL RANCH
COMMUNITY PARK

Glenn Ranch Rd.

Portola Pkwy.

Lake Forest

241

Mission
Viejo

El Toro Rd.

Lake Forest Dr.

Portola Pkwy.

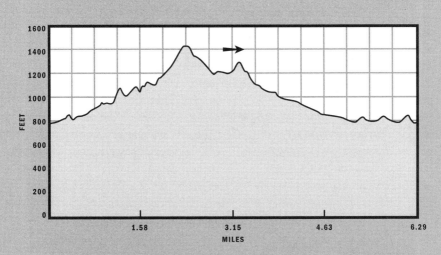

| 1600 |
| 1400 |
| 1200 |
| 1000 |
| 800 |
| 600 |
| 400 |
| 200 |
| 0 |

FEET

1.58   3.15   4.63   6.29

MILES

northeast). It's a fun and scenic trail and integral for any substantial ride in the small park. Therefore, the standard Whiting Ranch Loop begins at Portola and ends on or near Glenn Ranch Road.

Head down the sidewalk near Outback Steakhouse and cruise through the tunnel beneath Portola Parkway. Just past the tunnel, a connector trail leads to the entrance gate. Don't take this trail: it's a swampy mess. Ride up the pavement toward the parking lot and connect to the nicely groomed (and mud-free) trail that leads to the entrance gate.

Head up the Borrego Trail. You're bound to see plenty of other riders and hikers along this section. The wide singletrack runs beside the creek, slightly uphill, under a canopy of trees. Crank hard as the trail dips and weaves along the waterway and push hard over the short rocky rises. The trail widens as you head farther up the canyon. Past 1.5 miles stay right and follow Mustard Road to Four Corners. This is the longest straight climb of the ride, and it's not much—however the last third of a mile is fairly steep.

As the name suggests, there are a few options at Four Corners. A right turn leads to Dreaded Hill Road. Spur Road, directly left and uphill, connects to Santiago Canyon Road. If you want to add The Luge loop to this ride (another 7-plus miles), turn right on Santiago Canyon Road and then left up the Modjeska Grade to the Santiago Trail.

Foregoing the Luge option, continue straight at Four Corners and then make a quick right onto Whiting Road. Soon, at 2.4 miles, turn left on the Cactus Hill Trail. The singletrack winds down a razorback ridge, amid plenty of looming cacti, into a small, lushly foliated canyon. Near 2.8 miles fork left and climb the Sage Scrub Trail. It's a short, challenging climb, but push hard—it's the last significant climb of the ride.

At 3.2 miles turn right and continue on the Sage Scrub Trail. The concave singletrack winds sharply and somewhat steeply downhill. At trail's end, near 3.6 miles, merge back onto Whiting Road and continue cranking downhill. At 3.9 miles turn right and head across the Serrano Cow Trail, breezing through a grove of live oaks and coming to Serrano Road. Continue straight on Serrano Road, cruising the rest of the way out of the park. Just before the dirt road ends, a right fork on Serrano Road leads to Portola Parkway. Turn right onto the pavement at 5.3 miles and head back, through two stoplights, to the trailhead. Remember to use the tunnel to return to the parking lot instead of riding across the busy street.

After the Ride

Head down Portola Parkway and try something new at the Kuta Grille. The exotic restaurant serves American- and Asian-influenced cuisine in a setting that is pure South Pacific. Not what you'd expect to find in sterile Foothill Ranch. The food is fun, fresh, and fairly priced. Live it up!

The Kuta Grille
26772 Portola Parkway
Foothill Ranch, CA 92610
(949) 586-5882

CRYSTAL COVE STATE PARK AND LAGUNA WILDERNESS

EL MORRO CANYON LOOP

KEY AT-A-GLANCE INFORMATION

Length: 8.9 miles

Configuration: Loop with 0.4-mile out-and-back

Aerobic difficulty: A moderate, rolling climb punctuated with a couple of steep, difficult sections

Technical difficulty: Easy to moderate; majority of ride consists of fire roads. There are two well-worn singletrack sections and a steep plunge near the end of the loop. Ruts and silt on roads vary by season and may add to the difficulty.

Exposure: Complete sun on the ridge, minimal shade in the canyon except for a canopy of live oaks near the back of the canyon

Scenery: Rolling coastal canyon scrubland; ridgeline vistas offer one-of-a-kind ocean views.

Trail traffic: Moderate, but can be heavy on weekends

Riding time: 1–1.5 hours

Access: Parking at Crystal Cove State Park costs $10; the park is open 6 a.m.–sunset. During the winter you may want to call to check for rain closures. Rangers will ticket riders who use the park during closures.

GPS TRAILHEAD COORDINATES (WGS 84)

UTM Zone (WGS84) 11S
Easting 0423594
Northing 3714293
Latitude N 33°33'56.07"
Longitude W 117°49'23.50"

In Brief

The ride begins near the mouth of El Morro Canyon and follows the canyon to its terminus just above the San Joaquin Tollway. From the back of the canyon, a short jaunt on the Missing Link Trail leads to Morro Ridge Road. The ridge road bisects Emerald Canyon and El Morro Canyon as it heads back toward the Pacific Ocean. A final sharp descent back into El Morro Canyon allows for stunning coastline views. On clear days you will be able to see Palos Verdes, Catalina Island, and even distant San Clemente Island. Once you make it back to the canyon, turn left and complete the short climb back to the trailhead.

Information

Crystal Cove State Park
8471 Pacific Coast Highway
Laguna Beach, CA 92651
(949) 494-3539

Description

The first 200 yards run smooth and flat behind the former site of El Morro Trailer Park. From here the trail

DIRECTIONS

From O.C. North: take the CA 405 freeway south to the CA 73 freeway. Go south 5.2 miles to the Newport Coast Drive exit (toll required). Follow Newport Coast Drive 3.8 miles to CA 1 (Pacific Coast Highway). Go south on Pacific Coast Highway 1.2 miles and look for El Morro School. The fourth stoplight past Newport Coast is signed SCHOOL/STATE PARK. Turn left and follow the road behind the school to the Crystal Cove parking lot.

From O.C. South: Take the CA 405 freeway north to the CA 133 freeway (Laguna Canyon Road). Follow the road 8 miles to where it ends at CA 1 (Pacific Coast Highway). Turn right and go 2.7 miles on Pacific Coast Highway to the School/State Park stoplight. Turn right and follow the road behind the school to the Crystal Cove parking lot. The trailhead is on the ocean side of the parking lot.

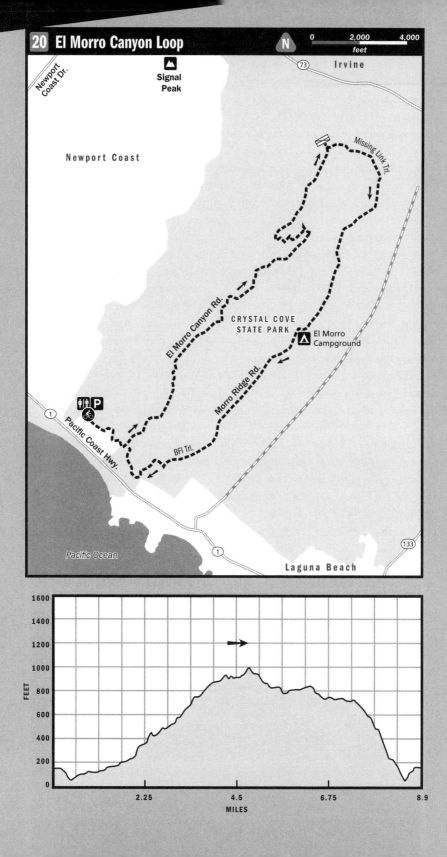

N

0   2,000   4,000
feet

Irvine

73

Signal
Peak

Newport
Coast Dr.

Newport Coast

Missing Link Trl.

El Morro Canyon Rd.

CRYSTAL COVE
STATE PARK

El Morro
Campground

Morro Ridge Rd.

Pacific Coast Hwy.

1

BFI Trl.

1

133

Pacific Ocean

Laguna Beach

1600

1400

1200

1000

800

FEET

600

400

200

0

2.25   4.5   6.75   8.9

MILES

quickly winds down into the canyon. This is an open section, but also fairly fast, so beware of hikers, especially around the two blind left-hand turns. At the bottom of the hill, the road dips across El Morro Creek. Don't expect to find water here except during the wet winter months. After large storms the creek sometimes brims with muddy water; however, the park will generally close until the water and mud subside.

Past the first creek crossing, sweeping grassy hills rise up to the ridgelines. Closer to the road lie the rusty remnants of strawberry fields, cultivated by Japanese Americans until the onset of World War II. Farther along, the canyon briefly narrows, and the road runs adjacent to the creek bed. This section tends to be well worn and rocky from winter washouts but is almost always rideable. After 0.8 miles the road crosses the creek again, and a short grind uphill reveals the widest section of the canyon. In the early spring, flowering mustard forms a magnificent yellow palette along these slopes. To the right is an old, washed-out earthen reservoir. Just past the reservoir the canyon road intersects two additional roads. Ascending to the right is the East Cut Across Road, informally named "I Think I Can," a long climb to Morro Ridge Road. On the left is Mach One, a straight, steep incline leading to No Name Ridge. Past the intersection, the road drops down and again runs just above creek level.

After a too-short flat section, the road veers left. This is where the climbing begins in earnest. At the 2-mile mark the trail turns abruptly upward. The first climb seems unremarkable and can be muscled through in most conditions. However, just past a culvert, the next climb offers a substantial challenge—a gut-busting, 100-foot elevation gain over 100 yards. The road originally followed a more sensible (and scenic) path closer to the base of the canyon, but the El Niño rains of the early 1990s damaged it. Park rangers closed the original route and redirected traffic up the arduous power-pole access road. Once finished wondering how the Edison people ever get their trucks up the incline, you may want to turn around and take in your first clear view of the Pacific Ocean. Past the crest of the climb, you can catch your breath as you coast back down into the canyon, but be aware of a completely blind turn at the bottom of the first hill.

Eventually, the power-pole route rejoins El Morro Canyon Road, leading into one of the most scenic sections of the park, a majestic grove of sycamores and oaks that line the upper creek. The tree canopy provides a perfect respite from the heat of the canyon. It's a nice place to take a break, especially since the biggest climb of the ride looms ahead. Near the 3-mile mark the road forks. Turn left and follow the West Loop, a 1.25-mile climb to the top of the canyon. The climb starts out fairly steep, then flattens as the road meanders back toward the ocean. After 0.4 miles the road hairpins toward a steep, bumpy climb, but crank hard knowing the most difficult part of the climb will soon be over.

Another 0.7 miles of rolling ridge climbing brings you to the top of the canyon. Head past the East Loop Road intersection to arrive at a gate. The gate leads to Laguna Coast Wilderness Park and will generally be open on weekends. Look for the Missing Link Trail directly to the right of the gate. Turn onto the trail and crank for 0.5 miles, winding through tight turns and dips. The trail culminates with a short, dusty climb to Photoman Point. On clear winter days, stand on the geological marker and you may be able to see downtown Los Angeles or San Diego's Point Loma. Even hazy days afford a view of the Saddleback Mountains.

From Photoman a short jaunt on a singletrack leads down to Morro Ridge Road. From here the way back is obvious as the ocean will nearly always be in view. Three quick roller-coaster drops give way to a flat section of road. Emerald Canyon lies to the southeast—look for deer and coyote darting up the steep precipice.

After a short, easy climb the road runs past the El Morro Ridge Campsite. From here follow the road downhill. "I Think I Can" goes right at the 6.7-mile mark, but stay left and keep heading toward the ocean. After 7.3 miles another road forks left toward Emerald Bay, but this time stay to the right, heading back toward El Morro Canyon. At the point where the road changes temporarily from dirt to pavement, the steep incline known as BFI begins—just be happy you are heading down and not up. Once the pavement ends be mindful of loose gravel on the road.

If you don't mind interrupting your descent, look to the left for a small roadside trail near the 7.8-mile mark. The trail leads to a concrete mound, below which is a small, inaccessible bunker, part of a network of bunkers built and manned during World War II. Today there aren't any enemy submarines, but the point affords great views of the Newport coastline.

Back on the road, follow it until it nears Pacific Coast Highway, then veer right onto the BFI Trail. The top section of the trail is fast and easy, but it soon turns right and drops fast and steep to El Morro Canyon. Watch for ruts and water boards on the steep section. Once you reach the canyon, turn left on El Morro Canyon Road and retrace the short climb back to the trailhead.

Crystal Cove State Park is popular with hikers, bird-watchers and, to a lesser degree, equestrians. There are several blind corners along the trails and roads. Be particularly mindful of others near the trailhead and at the base of the canyon.

Special note: El Morro is the given name of the region, referring to the headland just south of the park. The name is generally misspelled on maps as El Moro due to a county surveying error in the 1930s.

After the Ride

Since you've managed nearly 1,200 feet of total climbing, you may want to rejuvenate yourself with some beer and pizza at Gina's Pizza in Boat Canyon. The Laguna Beach location is just 3 miles south on Pacific Coast Highway.

Gina's Pizza
610 North Coast Highway
Laguna Beach, CA 92651
(949) 497-4421

RATTLESNAKE LOOP

KEY AT-A-GLANCE INFORMATION

KEY AT-A-GLANCE INFORMATION

Length: 8.5 miles

Configuration: Loop

Aerobic difficulty: Moderate except for a couple short, steep grinds

Technical difficulty: Rattlesnake downhill at the end of Red Tail Ridge requires advanced bike-handling skills. However, it is a short section and can be easily walked by novice riders and those disinclined to falling. The rest of the ride ranges from easy to moderate.

Exposure: Complete sun on ridges; El Morro Canyon has one shady section before the last climb.

Scenery: The sweeping coastal canyons are particularly lush and green in the springtime; the ridge-line offers panoramic ocean views.

Trail traffic: Moderate to heavy in the canyon, lighter on Red Tail Ridge.

Riding time: 1–1.5 hours

Access: Parking at Crystal Cove State Park costs $10; the park is open 6 a.m.–sunset. During the winter you may want to call to check for rain closures. Rangers will ticket riders who use the park during closures.

GPS TRAILHEAD COORDINATES (WGS 84)

UTM Zone (WGS84) 11S

Easting 0423594

Northing 3714293

Latitude N 33°33'56.07"

Longitude W 117°49'23.50"

In Brief

The first part of the loop is all fire road, rolling through scenic El Morro Canyon. At the back of the canyon, a mile-long grade ascends to the ridgeline. Continue along the fast and forgiving Fence Line Trail, cranking toward Red Tail Ridge. The path down Red Tail Ridge starts fast, narrows to a brush-lined singletrack, then ends with the rocky, rutted Rattlesnake descent. The trail dead-ends at a utility-pole access road that dips and then climbs to No Name Ridge. The ridge road rolls toward the ocean; a smooth, gradual descent ends just above the parking lot.

Information

Crystal Cove State Park
8471 Pacific Coast Highway
Laguna Beach, CA 92651
(949) 494-3539

Description

Begin behind the former location of El Morro Trailer Park. As of this writing it is a demolition site, but the state eventually plans to use the space as a campground/RV

DIRECTIONS

From O.C. North: take the CA 405 freeway south to the CA 73 freeway. Go south 5.2 miles to the Newport Coast Drive exit (toll required). Follow Newport Coast Drive 3.8 miles to CA 1 (Pacific Coast Highway). Go south on Pacific Coast Highway 1.2 miles and look for El Morro School. The fourth stoplight past Newport Coast is signed SCHOOL/STATE PARK. Turn left and follow the road behind the school to the Crystal Cove parking lot.

From O.C. South: Take the CA 405 freeway north to the CA 133 freeway (Laguna Canyon Road). Follow the road 8 miles to where it ends at CA 1 (Pacific Coast Highway). Turn right and go 2.7 miles on Pacific Coast Highway to the School/State Park stoplight. The trailhead is on the ocean side of the parking lot.

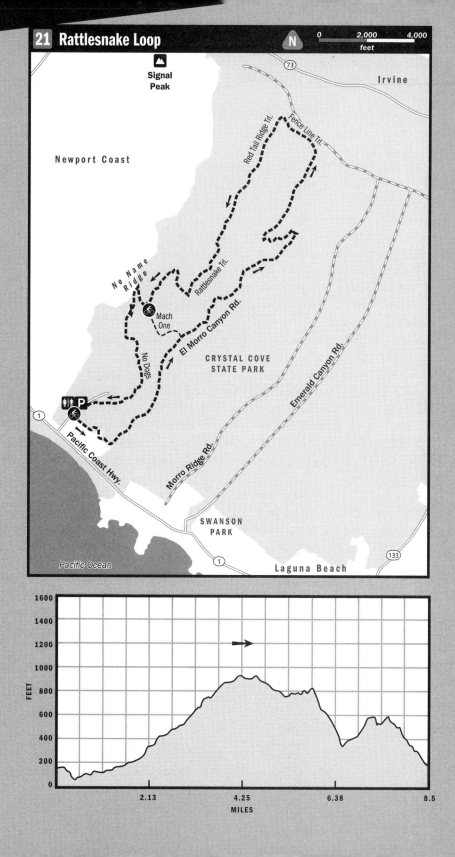

N

0   2,000   4,000
feet

Signal
Peak

Irvine

73

Newport Coast

Red Tail Ridge Trl.

Fence Line Trl.

No Name
Ridge

Rattlesnake Trl.

Mach
One

El Morro Canyon Rd.

No Dogs

CRYSTAL COVE
STATE PARK

Emerald Canyon Rd.

P

1

Pacific Coast Hwy.

Morro Ridge Rd.

SWANSON
PARK

1

133

Pacific Ocean

Laguna Beach

FEET

1600
1400
1200
1000
800
600
400
200
0

2.13   4.25   6.38   8.5
MILES

park. After a short stretch the road drops down into the canyon, crossing El Morro Creek at the bottom of the descent. This is a heavily trafficked section, so be mindful of hikers and other bikers.

The base of the canyon runs generally level and offers ample opportunity to warm up. The first climbs are short and sweet—quick intervals followed by short downhills. At 1.4 miles two roads join El Morro Canyon Road. On the right, the East Cut Across Road, informally named "I Think I Can," climbs to Morro Ridge and, on the left, Mach One heads straight up to No Name Ridge. Continue cranking up the canyon. After another easy rolling section, the road climbs in two steep intervals. The second of these climbs is particularly steep and silty. It comes at the 2.2-mile mark and follows a utility-pole access road (the original route along the canyon road was lost after a particularly nasty El Niño winter). The climb is a gut buster, but when you reach the power pole, you'll be rewarded with a sweeping view of the canyon below.

The route drops back into the canyon, coursing through a canopy of live oak and sycamore trees. This is the only significant shade of the ride. There are also some nice, if not remarkable, caves in this section, but beware of poison oak.

At 2.9 miles the road forks, but both options lead to the same destination. Head left, ascending on the more forgiving West Loop route. The climb runs initially toward the ocean. After a hairpin the moderate grade turns momentarily steep, ascending to the ridgeline. Follow the ridgeline another rolling 0.8 miles, and you've reached the apex of the ride.

Past the junction of the East Loop and the West Loop, a gate separates Crystal Cove State Park from Laguna Coast Wilderness Park. Veer left at the gate and crank along the Fence Line Trail. This is a good warm-up singletrack—smooth and flat with fast, tight turns. At 4.6 miles the Fence Line Trail T-bones into the Red Tail Ridge Trail; here turn left and head toward the ocean.

Red Tail Ridge Trail begins as a fire road and runs generally downhill, although not steeply. If you're not going too fast, at 4.7 miles you'll notice a small footpath on the left. The footpath leads to a formation of rocks and caves that bare an archaeological record of the indigenous Chumash Indians (although no official mention is made of this in the park literature).

At 4.9 miles a second fire road veers right and heads to Deer Canyon. Continue straight along the ridge. The road soon narrows, and the Rattlesnake singletrack begins. The first section is fast and level, carved between dense scrub. After a short, rocky drop the trail climbs to the head of the ridge. Near the 6-mile mark the trail drops somewhat steeply. This is the only technically difficult part of the ride, a rutted descent through a garden of boulders the size of small kitchen appliances. Over the years the trail has widened a bit as riders have looked for new lines, but they are all pretty much equally bad. The best bet for cleaning the trail is not to worry too much about your line, just keep your momentum and your confidence as you bounce down the rocks. If your bike does not have ample suspension, you might try walking.

After the rattling descent, the trail dead-ends into another utility-pole access road. Head right, the road drops down quickly, then climbs gradually until it intersects Mach

One. Turn right and grind uphill. After 300 yards Mach One dead ends into No Name Ridge. This section of the park briefly appeared in the Jack Nicholson film drama, *A Few Good Men*. Someone apparently felt that the state park resembled Guantanamo Bay. That was, of course, before 800 Mediterranean-style homes were built on the ridges of nearby Newport Coast.

Turn left on No Name Ridge. The ridge route roller coasters, so use momentum from the down section to push through the short incline. At 7.6 miles the road veers left and heads gradually downhill. This grade, listed as No Dogs on the park map, heads directly back to the parking lot. The last downhill runs smooth and fast with fairly forgiving turns. It's tempting to let loose on this section, but be aware of hikers, particularly around the blind right-hand turns.

Crystal Cove State Park is popular with hikers, bird-watchers and, to a lesser degree, equestrians. There are several blind corners along the trails and roads. Be particularly mindful of others near the trailhead and at the base of the canyon.

Special note: El Morro is the given name of the region, referring to the headland just south of the park. The name is generally misspelled on maps as El Moro due to a county surveying error in the 1930s.

After the Ride

Head up to the Shake Shack, sit on the wooden deck, and enjoy the view. It's about 2 miles north on the ocean side of Pacific Coast Highway. You can't turn left into the driveway, so you'll need to go to the stoplight at Los Trancos and make a U-turn. If you have more time, you might try The Beachcomber restaurant at Crystal Cove. In that case, head into the Los Trancos parking lot and take the shuttle down to the cove. The restaurant is right on the sand, among the beach shacks. You can imagine what it was like to live in this idyllic community before the state evicted all the residents and turned the shanty beach houses into overnight rentals.

Crystal Cove Shake Shack
7703 East Coast Highway
Newport Beach, CA 92657
(949) 497-9666

22

EMERALD CANYON

KEY AT-A-GLANCE INFORMATION

Length: 12.4 miles

Configuration: Out-and-back with a small loop at the end

Aerobic difficulty: A steep climb at the outset will test most rider's mettle. The second climb is more forgiving.

Technical difficulty: Mostly moderate aside from two rutted and bumpy downhill singletrack sections; the trail through Emerald Canyon requires a modest amount of bushwhacking.

Exposure: Complete sun on the ridge but good shade in canyon

Scenery: The canyon is lush and unspoiled; the ridgelines offer fantastic views of the Laguna Beach coastline.

Trail traffic: Light

Riding time: 2 hours

Access: Free street parking. Laguna Coast Wilderness Park is open daily, 7 a.m.–sunset. The park is subject to closure during rainy weather.

Special comments: Be respectful of the residents when parking on the street.

GPS TRAILHEAD COORDINATES (WGS 84)

UTM Zone (WGS84)   11S

Easting   426067

Northing 3712615

Latitude   N 33°33'02"

Longitude   W 117°47'47"

In Brief

A steep ascent at the outset eventually leads to Bommer Ridge Road. After 2.5 miles a bumpy, singletrack descent lands you in Emerald Canyon. This is the crux of the ride—an out-and-back cruise through the Laguna Coast Wilderness Park's finest, and least visited, canyon. A fast ride down the canyon is punctuated with tight turns and short, rolling descents. The return trip affords plenty of time to enjoy the scenery. A fairly forgiving climb out of Emerald Canyon leads back to Bommer Ridge. The return retraces the original ridge route, then diverts toward Allview Terrace, dropping down along a fence-line singletrack. A short jaunt on residential streets leads back to Dartmoor Street.

Information

Laguna Coast Wilderness Park
20101 Laguna Canyon Road
Laguna Beach, CA 92651
(949) 923-2235

DIRECTIONS

From O.C. North: Take the CA 405 freeway south to the CA 73 freeway. Go south 6.6 miles and exit at Newport Coast Drive (toll required). Merge right and continue 3.8 miles to CA 1 (Pacific Coast Highway). Go south on Pacific Coast Highway toward Laguna Beach. After 3.6 miles turn left on San Joaquin Drive. At the top of the hill, turn right on Hillcrest Drive. Take the first left onto Dartmoor Street and follow it up the hill; the trailhead is at the end of the street.

From O.C. South: Take the CA 405 freeway north to the CA 133 freeway (Laguna Canyon Road). Follow the road 8 miles till it ends at CA 1 (Pacific Coast Highway). Go north on Pacific Coast Highway 1 mile and turn right on Viejo Street. At the top of the hill, turn left on Hillcrest Drive and then immediately right on Dartmoor Street. Follow Dartmoor Street up the hill; the trailhead is at the end of the street.

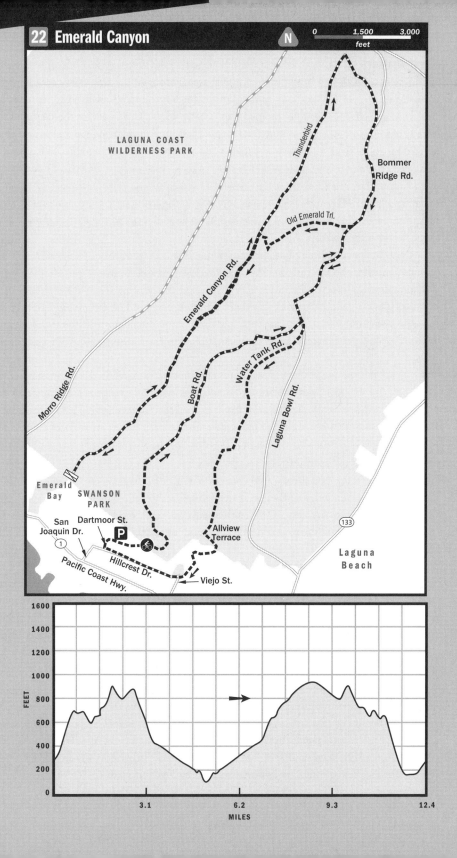

N

0   1,500   3,000
feet

LAGUNA COAST
WILDERNESS PARK

Thunderbird

Bommer
Ridge Rd.

Old Emerald Trl.

Emerald Canyon Rd.

Morro Ridge Rd.

Boat Rd.

Water Tank Rd.

Laguna Bowl Rd.

Emerald
Bay

SWANSON
PARK

San
Joaquin Dr.

Dartmoor St.

P

Hillcrest Dr.

Pacific Coast Hwy.

1

Viejo St.

Allview
Terrace

133

Laguna
Beach

1600
1400
1200
1000
800
600
400
200
0

FEET

3.1   6.2   9.3   12.4
MILES

Description

Climb past Gate 18 and head out on a gravel access road. At the first curve stay right and keep heading uphill. The climb is long and hard, but the views of the Laguna coastline are unparalleled. After a mile the road temporarily levels. This is where the Laguna Coast Wilderness begins in earnest. Narrow, steep-walled Emerald Canyon lies below and to the west. The gravel road soon gives way to dirt and continues up the ridgeline. The rolling ascent, punctuated with a couple of short, steep grades, finally ends where Boat Road merges with Laguna Bowl Road. Here, after 2 miles of hard climbing, you can rest assured that the most trying part of the ride is complete and bask in the panoramic view—Emerald Canyon lies to the west, Laguna Canyon to the south, and Saddleback to the east. Bommer Ridge Road lies directly ahead.

Continue heading inland on Bommer Ridge Road. The fire road drops briefly and then climbs gently. At the 2.6-mile mark, follow the Old Emerald Trail as it veers left. Be watchful: although well worn, the trail is easy to miss (at this writing there is a sign only at the bottom). The singletrack initially runs back toward the ocean. The descent is fast, steep, and bumpy; watch out for loose rocks, ruts, and cacti. After a hairpin turn the trail levels and winds through the canyon foliage. Past a small bridge the trail intersects Emerald Canyon Road.

Turn left at Emerald Canyon Road and head toward the ocean. You'll immediately notice that it isn't a road at all. What used to be a fire road has changed to a singletrack trail after years without grading. The trail down is fun, fast, and relatively easy. However, be aware of branches and bushes that protrude onto the trail; gloves are a necessity and long sleeves might be in order for the scratch sensitive. In the springtime seasonal growth will make some parts of the trail tricky to negotiate.

At 4.7 miles the road turns left to cross a creek. Be careful not to miss the turn: it comes after a fairly fast section, and there is a steep drop on the right side of the road. The creek itself is easily crossed and usually dry, although it may have a splash of water in the winter months. Past the creek the road continues for another 0.2 miles and then dead-ends at the community of Emerald Bay.

A sturdy gate and fence block access to the streets of posh Emerald Bay, but fret not, the ride out of the canyon is far from difficult. Going slower, you will more fully experience the flora and fauna that were merely a blur on the way down. Canopies of live oaks cover the narrow sections of the canyon where deer, coyotes, and roadrunners are all frequent visitors. Dense foliage abounds throughout the canyon. In 1993, when wildfires ravaged Laguna Beach, the lush plant life of Emerald Canyon provided plentiful fuel for the wind-driven firestorm. Flames raged into Emerald Bay and took several homes.

Past the intersection of the Old Emerald Trail, continue riding out of the canyon. The singletrack eventually widens to a fire road, aptly named Thunderbird by local riders who enjoy its high-speed descents. Thankfully, the climb up Thunderbird is fairly forgiving—after two initial short, steep grinds, the grade mellows to a rolling middle-gear push. At 8 miles Thunderbird dead-ends into Bommer Ridge Road. Turn right and head back toward the ocean. The next 2 miles are nominally uphill but fast and easy.

Marko cranking up Emerald Canyon

Near the 10-mile mark, you'll pass the fork to Boat Road. Continue straight over a small crest for about 50 yards and at the next fork go right to Water Tank Road. Follow the ridge; the descent is gradual but fast and wide open. At 10.6 miles a dead-end road veers up and to the left. Stay right on the lower road. After a short climb you'll reach a barbed-wire fence with an open gate. Go through the gate and head immediately right down a fence-line singletrack. The trail is rutted and rocky, and be careful of cacti and barbed wire. Eventually the trail turns left and runs behind a fenced residential neighborhood. Continue downhill to where the trail cuts right, through an opening in the fence. Turn left on Allview Terrace and head downhill to a gate. The gate is easily passable, but if you want it to open for you, just lay your bike on the ground to trigger the magnetic mechanism. Turn right on High Drive and then continue right on Hillcrest Drive. Follow Hillcrest 0.5 miles back to Dartmoor Street.

After the Ride

Head to downtown Laguna. Among your many eating options is La Sirena, serving up tasty and affordable Mexican cuisine. Sit outside, and you might be able to catch a glimpse of some of the climbs you just mastered.

La Sirena

347 Mermaid Street

Laguna Beach, CA 92651

(949) 499-2301

|LAGUNA RIDGE LOOP

Length: 5.8 miles

Configuration: Loop

Aerobic difficulty: Moderate; one steep climb at the outset.

Technical difficulty: Difficult; the Laguna Ridge Trail has some dicey rock gardens, steep sections, and a couple of rock drops.

Exposure: Complete sun

Scenery: Great coastline and canyon views

Trail traffic: Light to moderate; the greatest concentration is on Boat Road.

Riding time: 1 hour

Access: Free street parking is available on Dartmoor Street in North Laguna. The entire ride takes place in the Laguna Coast Wilderness Park. The park is open daily, 7 a.m.–sunset but is subject to closure during rainy weather.

Special comments: Be respectful of the residents when parking on the street.

GPS TRAILHEAD COORDINATES (WGS 84)
UTM Zone (WGS84)   11S
Easting   426067
Northing   3712615
Latitude   N 33°33'02"
Longitude   W 117°47'47"

In Brief

Past the gate at Dartmoor, Boat Road is a steep route to the ridgeline. Crank up the gravel road, then follow the dirt road along the ridgeline. The climb ends where Boat Road and two other fire roads merge into Bommer Ridge Road. This is also the point where the Laguna Ridge Trail begins. Drop straight down the rocky trail toward Laguna Canyon. Half way down, turn left on T and A. Follow the steep, technical singletrack all the way to Laguna Canyon Road. Turn right on the road and then ride the streets through North Laguna back to Dartmoor Street.

Information

Laguna Coast Wilderness Park
20101 Laguna Canyon Road
Laguna Beach, CA 92651
(949) 923-2235

Description

In the early days of mountain biking, before bikes had suspension, Laguna was legendary for its hard-core biking

DIRECTIONS

From O.C. North: Take the CA 405 freeway south to the CA 73 freeway. Go south 6.6 miles and exit at Newport Coast Drive (toll required). Merge right and continue 3.8 miles to CA 1 (Pacific Coast Highway). Go south on Pacific Coast Highway toward Laguna Beach. After 3.6 miles turn left on San Joaquin Drive. At the top of the hill, turn right on Hillcrest Drive. Dartmoor Street is the first street on the left. Follow Dartmoor Street up the hill; the trailhead is at the end of the street.

From O.C. South: Take the CA 405 freeway north to the CA 133 freeway (Laguna Canyon Road). Follow the road 8 miles till it ends at Pacific Coast Highway. Go north on Pacific Coast Highway 1 mile and turn right on Viejo Street. At the top of the hill, turn left on Hillcrest Drive and then immediately right on Dartmoor Street. Follow Dartmoor Street up the hill; the trailhead is at the end of the street.

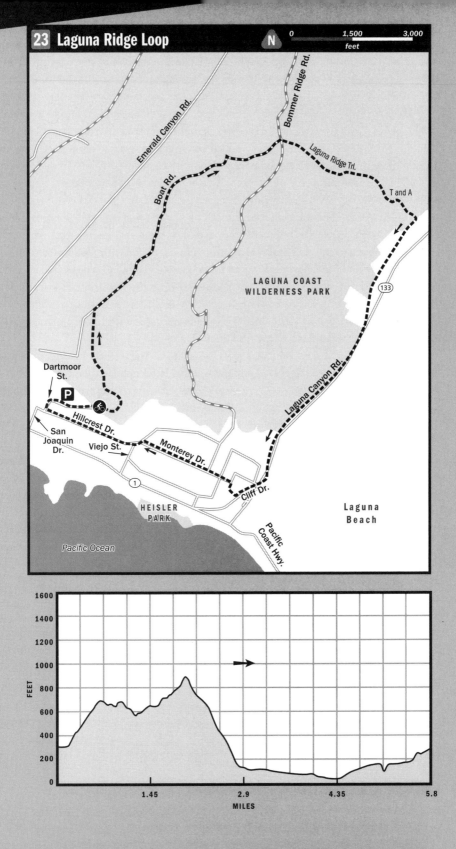

N

0   1,500   3,000
feet

Emerald Canyon Rd.

Bommer Ridge Rd.

Laguna Ridge Trl.

Boat Rd.

T and A

LAGUNA COAST
WILDERNESS PARK

133

Dartmoor
St.

P

Laguna Canyon Rd.

San
Joaquin
Dr.

Hillcrest Dr.

Viejo St.

Monterey Dr.

Cliff Dr.

Laguna
Beach

HEISLER
PARK

1

Pacific
Coast
Hwy.

Pacific Ocean

1600
1400
1200
1000
800
600
400
200
0

FEET

1.45   2.9   4.35   5.8
MILES

community. The local canyon topography allowed for the creation of steep, technical trails. A dedicated group of local riders built, rode, and maintained an amazing network of trails. But since most of the trails were on private land, it was a fairly covert operation.

These days most of the Laguna backcountry is open to the public. This is a good thing, of course, but use of the local open space has changed from the old covert days. Many of the old trails have been closed or have succumbed to foliage. However, a few of the classic trails remain. Downhillers, with their super suspension bikes, push the limits on many of these trails. This is particularly true on the south side of the canyon, where riders can car shuttle to Top of the World. The Laguna Ridge Trail is a great trail for riders who still want to use their legs to climb. The trail, with its offshoot T and A, was first blazed by mountain bikers in the early 1980s. Today the trail is in great shape and more challenging than ever.

This loop recalls the old school of Laguna mountain biking with a hard, steep climb followed by a steep, technical drop. However, the route could be merely considered a template for several possible rides in the area. Dartmoor Street is a somewhat arbitrary starting point, but a good one. You could just as easily begin at Willow Canyon Road or at Laguna Bowl Road. The loop may also be augmented with additional drops and climbs. Emerald Canyon or the Lizard Trail would both be great additions to the ride.

From Dartmoor Street, crank up a gravel access road. You'll reach the ridge after a continuous half-mile of climbing. Head straight on Boat Road into Laguna Coast Wilderness Park. The dirt road drops then climbs in short spurts along the rolling ridge. Scenic Emerald Canyon lies below to the left. Past 1.7 miles charge up the final grade on Boat Road. The climb ends at the intersection of three fire roads—here Boat Road, Water Tank Road, and Laguna Bowl Road all merge into Bommer Ridge Road.

The Laguna Ridge Trail begins about 50 feet south of where Boat Road and Bommer Ridge Road converge. Make the short climb to the top of the trail and then drop. The top section of the trail descends through a garden of small rocks and ruts. Keep your speed and bounce your way down. Maintaining momentum is the only way to make the trail.

After the first plunge, the trail levels somewhat and heads along a rounded ridge. At 2.3 miles drop left down T and A. This offshoot trail immediately plummets down a grassy hillside, then winds into the brush. The first, and largest, rock drop comes after a sharp lefthand turn. Farther down, the trail courses through a shoot of smaller rocks and ledges. The final drop, beneath a weathered tree, comes near the bottom of the trail.

At 2.8 miles pass through a gap in a fence and head right on Laguna Canyon Road. Ride down the canyon, and at 4.3 miles, veer right on Cliff Drive. Ride to the stop sign and then make successive right turns on Rosa Bonheur Street and Cypress Drive. Take the first left, on Monterey Drive, and follow it all the way to High Drive. Turn left and then immediately right on Hillcrest Drive. Near 5.5 miles turn right on Dartmoor Street and make the final climb to complete the ride.

DEER CANYON LOOP

KEY AT-A-GLANCE INFORMATION

Length: 7.1 miles

Configuration: Loop

Aerobic difficulty: Moderate except for a few short, grueling climbs

Technical difficulty: Varied; the Deer Canyon trail offers a few substantial technical challenges. Everything else is comparatively easy.

Exposure: Mostly complete sun

Scenery: Rolling coastal-canyon scrubland; ocean and Saddleback views

Trail traffic: Moderate but can be heavy on weekends

Riding time: 1–1.5 hours

Access: Free parking is available on Ridge Park Road atop Newport Coast. The majority of the ride takes place in Crystal Cove State Park.

Special comments: Crystal Cove State Park is often considered a mountain bike park. However, particularly on weekends, there are plenty of hikers on the trails. Be careful and respectful when riding in the park.

GPS TRAILHEAD COORDINATES (WGS 84)

UTM Zone (WGS84)   11S
Easting   0425630
Northing   3718740
Latitude   N 33°36'21"
Longitude   W 117°48'06"

In Brief

The excitement begins immediately on this loop. Starting atop Newport Coast, drop down the fun and challenging Deer Canyon Trail and ride it out all the way to the picnic tables at Deer Canyon. A steep climb up Ticketron leads to No Name Ridge. Follow the roller-coaster ridge road toward the ocean. Then turn left on the appropriately named Mach One and scream down to El Morro Canyon. Ride the dirt road up El Morro all the way back to the top of the canyon. A winding traverse on the Fence Line Trail and a short climb up Bommer Ridge Road complete the loop.

Information

Crystal Cove State Park
8471 Pacific Coast Highway
Laguna Beach, CA 92651
(949) 494-3539

Description

Ridge Park Road atop Newport Coast provides yet another access point to El Morro Canyon and the Laguna Coast Wilderness. This trailhead provides a nice option for riders coming from Irvine or central Orange County—it saves

DIRECTIONS

From the intersection of the CA 55 and CA 73 freeways: Take CA 73 south to MacArthur Boulevard. Merge onto MacArthur Boulevard and continue straight for 2.4 miles. Turn left on San Joaquin Hills Road and go 2.6 miles until the road ends at Newport Coast Drive. Turn right on Newport Coast Drive and take the first left on Ridge Park Road. Go straight and uphill for 1.5 miles. The trailhead is just beyond the cul-de-sac at road's end.

From Pacific Coast Highway: Head uphill on Newport Coast Drive 2.4 miles to Ridge Park Road. Turn right on Ridge Park Road. Go straight and uphill for 1.5 miles. The trailhead is just beyond the cul-de-sac at road's end.

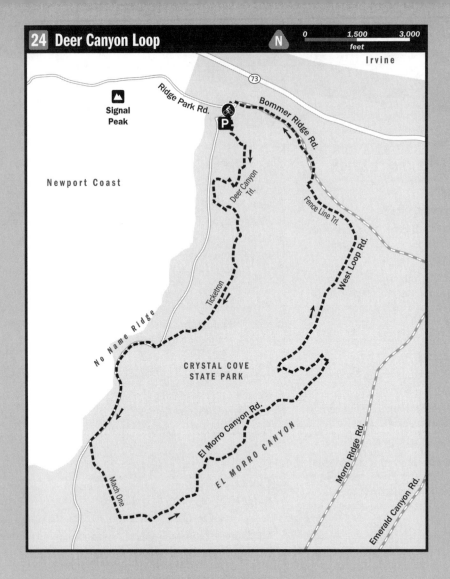

0   1,500   3,000
feet

N

Irvine

Signal Peak

Ridge Park Rd.

73

Bommer Ridge Rd.

Newport Coast

Deer Canyon Trl.

Fence Line Trl.

West Loop Rd.

Ticketon

No Mame Ridge

CRYSTAL COVE STATE PARK

El Morro Canyon Rd.

EL MORRO CANYON

Morro Ridge Rd.

Mach One

Emerald Canyon Rd.

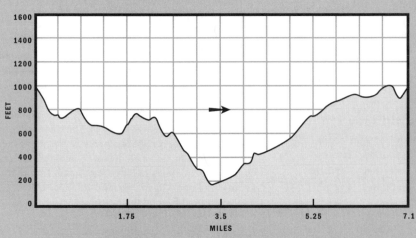

1600
1400
1200
1000
800
600
400
200
0

FEET

1.75   3.5   5.25   7.1
MILES

driving time and the $10 to park at Crystal Cove State Park. The minor disadvantage of the Ridge Park trailhead is the high starting elevation. Any loop from this trailhead starts with a drop and ends with a climb. Of course, you do have the option of parking at the bottom of Ridge Park Road and beginning your ride with a road climb.

Slip through the gate at road's end and head immediately right, down an unnamed county trail. Before you can even get your seat warm, at less than 0.1 mile, turn left and head down the Deer Canyon Trail. The most technical portion of the singletrack, a few midsize rock drops, comes fairly quickly. Near 0.2 miles the trail courses across a section of slick rock. Stay high and left over the first two rocks and then veer right and drop down to the right of the third rock. The trail continues down to, and then follows, a creek bed at the base of the canyon. Be ready for a couple of quick climbs and then, at 1.6 miles, a more substantial climb back toward the ridge. Before you get to the ridge, the trail levels and traverses the hillside before dropping down again toward the base of the canyon. Eventually the singletrack runs out at the Deer Canyon picnic area.

Past 1.3 miles turn right onto Ticketron. The well-worn trail follows the canyon for a spell and then climbs sharply in two consecutive intervals. The first interval is brutal but makeable. The second interval, just as steep and longer, is often too loose to climb. Atop the hill, at 1.9 miles, head left on No Name Ridge. The ridge road alternately drops and climbs. Push hard on the downhill sections and use your momentum to carry you up the hills.

At 2.7 miles turn left on Mach One. They don't call it Mach One for nothing—it's a straight, fast shot all the way down to El Morro Canyon. Follow the left fork of the road just before you reach the bottom and then head left on El Morro Canyon Road.

The canyon road runs flat for a while and then begins to climb in a series of short, steep hills. The hardest climb comes at 4.1 miles, a gut-busting grind up a utility-pole grade (the original, and less steep, road was washed out and closed after the El Niño rains of the 1990s).

Past a grove of live oaks, at 4.7 miles, fork left onto the West Loop Road. This is the final climb to the top of the canyon. It's a gradual grade, so strong climbers will be able to make much of the hill in the middle chainring. The steepest section comes directly after the road hairpins away from the ocean. The final part of the climb lopes along the ridge all the way to the back boundary of the state park.

At 6 miles veer left at the gate onto the Fence Line Trail. Crank through the turns till the trail runs out at Red Tail Ridge. Turn right on the dirt road and head down to the gate. Past the gate, at 6.4 miles, head left on Bommer Ridge Road. And that's it—two short climbs up Bommer complete the loop.

After the Ride

Drive down Ridge Park Road to Newport Coast Drive and into Newport Coast Shopping Center. Among the restaurants in the center is Zov's Café, Bakery, and Bar. Zov's offers Mediterranean cuisine and great sandwiches on fresh-baked breads. The cookies are pretty good too.

Zov's
Newport Coast Shopping Center, 2123 Newport Coast Drive
Newport Beach, CA 92657
(949) 760-9687

25

NIX NATURE CENTER SHUTTLE RIDE (WITH LOOP OPTION)

KEY AT-A-GLANCE INFORMATION

KEY AT-A-GLANCE INFORMATION

Length: 9.9 miles

Configuration: Shuttle ride

Aerobic difficulty: Moderate; several short ups and downs in the first 5 miles

Technical difficulty: Moderate; the Stage Coach Trail has some tight switchbacks, and much of the Lizard Trail runs thick with foliage.

Exposure: Complete sun for the majority of the ride. Most of the shade comes along the Lizard Trail.

Scenery: Laguna Canyon views, Irvine Ranch views, lush foliage, ocean views

Trail traffic: Light except for Willow Canyon Road

Riding time: 1.25–2 hours

Access: The Nix Nature Center is open daily, 9 a.m.–4 p.m. Parking costs $3. The entire ride takes place in Laguna Coast Wilderness Park.

Special comments: Stage Coach Trail is the only Nix Nature Center trail open to mountain biking. All other trails are for hiking only.

GPS TRAILHEAD COORDINATES (WGS 84)

UTM Zone (WGS84)   11S

Easting   0429191

Northing   3718918

Latitude   N 33°36'28"

Longitude   W 117°45'48"

In Brief

This ride begins at the Nix Nature Center in Laguna Canyon and ends at Shaw's Cove in north Laguna Beach. Optionally, you may also loop back to the Nix Nature Center.

Follow the Stage Coach Trail, climbing then dropping to Camarillo Canyon Road. Turn right and climb up to Serrano Ridge Road. Turn left and crank down Serrano Ridge Road until it forks. Head left and beneath the CA 73 toll road to Upper Laurel Canyon. Eventually you will reach the Lizard Trail, where you turn right and follow the tight singletrack all the way to Bommer Ridge Road. From here you have three options: (1) follow the ridge— via Bommer Ridge and Water Tank roads—all the way to north Laguna Beach and Shaw's Cove; (2) head down Willow Canyon Road to Laguna Canyon and ride the pavement back to the Nix Nature Center; (3) drop back down to Upper Laurel Canyon and retrace the beginning of the ride back to the Nix Nature Center.

Information

James and Rosemary Nix Nature Center
18751 Laguna Canyon Road
Laguna Beach, CA 92651

DIRECTIONS

From the intersection of the CA 405 and CA 133 freeways: Take CA 133 (Laguna Canyon Road) south toward Laguna Beach. Continue through the canyon for 3.6 miles and turn right at the Nix Nature Center entrance. Head through a gate and continue 0.2 miles to the parking area.

From the intersection of CA 1 (Pacific Coast Highway) and CA 133: Take Broadway Avenue and continue straight as it becomes CA 133 (Laguna Canyon Road) After 5 miles, look for a left-turn lane. Turn left across the southbound lanes of CA 133, head through a gate, and continue 0.2 miles to the Nix Nature Center parking lot.

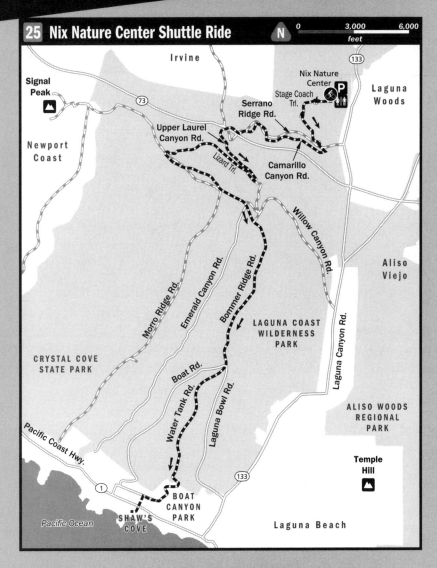

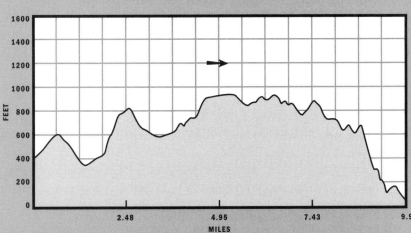

A view of Upper Laurel Canyon from the Lizard Trail

Laguna Coast Wilderness Park
20101 Laguna Canyon Road
Laguna Beach, CA 92651
(949) 923-2235

Description

The Nix Nature Center is the newest addition to Laguna Coast Wilderness Park. Opened in March of 2007, the stately building lies near Laguna Canyon Road among miles of previously inaccessible trails. Unfortunately, most of the trails are not open to mountain biking. The one exception is the Stage Coach Trail, a newly constructed singletrack that runs parallel to and above Laguna Canyon. Luckily, the Stage Coach Trail is well worth riding—scenic and chock full of challenging, tight switchbacks.

Grind up the Stage Coach Trail from the parking lot. It's a small climb—only 200 feet—but the switchbacks will test your skills and keep your attention. After about 0.5 miles the trail tops out and then winds down to Camarillo Canyon Road.

Near 1.3 miles turn right on Camarillo Canyon Road. The road runs fairly level for a spell and then turns impossibly steep as it approaches Serrano Ridge. Don't worry, the steep section is short-lived. Serrano Ridge Road comes as a reprieve at 2.2 miles; here turn left and head toward the toll road. You'll notice Shady Canyon below and to the north. This is part of the Irvine Ranch Land Reserve, and as several signs will tell you, it is only open to the public via docent-led tours.

Serrano Ridge Road splits after a short climb. Fork left, riding beneath the toll road, onto Upper Laurel Canyon Road. Drop down the grade and follow the tree-lined road through the upper canyon. Near 3.3 miles Upper Laurel Canyon Road ends, becoming Laurel Canyon Road. The downhill section (left turn) is open only to hiking. Fork right, but before heading uphill, turn right again on the Lizard Trail. Crank up the narrow singletrack, winding through live oaks and chaparral. It's a fun trail, and the dense canopy of foliage will make you forget that the toll road looms nearby.

The last section of the Lizard Trail climbs up to Bommer Ridge Road. Turn left, at 4.5 miles, and cruise along the dirt road just outside the boundary of Crystal Cove State Park. You have several options at this point. If you want to return to the Nix Nature Center, fork left on Willow Canyon Road at 5.5 miles. From Willow Canyon Road, you may either turn left, after another 0.2 miles, and follow a connector road back to Laurel Canyon Road (and then backtrack to the Nix Nature Center); or you may continue straight to Laguna Canyon Road. It's a little more than a mile downhill to the canyon floor and then 1.3 miles on the road back to the Nix Nature Center.

To complete the shuttle ride, fork right at 5.5 miles and stay on Bommer Ridge Road. Follow the undulating ridge. After a short, steep climb, the road reaches a double fork at 7.5 miles. Take the second right on Water Tank Road. Continue down the ridge, ripping along the fast, open section. Be sure to fork right again at 8.2 miles, then crank up one last steep climb to a gate. At 8.6 miles turn right on a fence-line singletrack. Bounce down the fun trail and then veer right, near 8.9 miles, onto pavement.

Continue left and downhill on Allview Terrace Road. At 9.2 miles turn right on High Drive. Follow the road downhill and curve right onto Hillcrest Drive. Turn left on Wave Street, at 9.6 miles, and head downhill to Pacific Coast Highway. Cross the highway and continue to Cliff Drive. Turn right on Cliff Drive—the steps to Shaw's Cove, the endpoint of the ride, will be almost immediately on the left.

After the Ride

It's no accident the ride ends at Shaw's Cove—this is one of the nicest beaches in Laguna. If the weather is warm, secure your bike in a safe spot and wash off some of the dirt in the ocean. Then, if you're hungry (and thirsty), head to downtown Laguna and check out the Ocean Avenue Restaurant and Brewery. The streetside patio is a perfect place to relax and to enjoy a handcrafted beer with a plateful of hearty Italian cuisine.

Ocean Avenue Restaurant and Brewery
237 Ocean Avenue
Laguna Beach, CA 92651
(949) 497-3381

THE LIZARD TRAIL

In Brief

The first 2 miles are all climbing, following Willow Canyon Road to Bommer Ridge Road to the back of Crystal Cove State Park. Hop into the state park and head down the Missing Link Trail. Continue on the Fence Line Trail, finally ending up at Red Tail Ridge. Head through the gate back to Bommer Ridge Road and backtrack 100 yards to the Lizard Trail. The Lizard Trail drops into Laurel Canyon and follows a tight, twisting course through dense foliage. Past the trail, a short climb on a fire road brings you back to the top of Willow Canyon Road. The last 1.4 miles of the ride is all downhill, fast and fun, straight back to the parking lot.

KEY AT-A-GLANCE INFORMATION

Length: 6.1 miles

Configuration: 3.3-mile loop with 2.8-mile out-and-back

Aerobic difficulty: Moderate; the hardest climbing is right at the beginning.

Technical difficulty: Generally moderate; the singletrack is a bit rutty and requires plenty of bushwhacking, but there are few, if any, steep technical sections.

Exposure: Partial to full sun on the ridge; the Lizard Trail offers plenty of shade.

Scenery: Coastal canyon views, ocean views, and macro views of dense canyon flora

Trail traffic: Moderate to light

Riding time: 1–1.25 hours

Access: Laguna Coast Wilderness Park is open daily, 7 a.m.–sunset. The parking lot on Laguna Canyon Road (just south of CA 73) is open daily, 8 a.m.–4 p.m. Parking costs $3. If the lot is full, look for street parking on Laguna Canyon Road.

Information

Laguna Coast Wilderness Park
20101 Laguna Canyon Road
Laguna Beach, CA 92651
(949) 923-2235

Description

You may want to consider a warm-up spin on Laguna Canyon Road, since there is little, if any, time for warming up between the trailhead and the first climb. At the base of Willow Canyon, look for friendly park docents sitting next to the prefab buildings, give them your name, and be on your way. The ride begins in a serene

GPS TRAILHEAD COORDINATES (WGS 84)

UTM Zone (WGS84)   11S
Easting   0429205
Northing   3715843
Latitude   N 33°34'38"
Longitude   W 117°45'46"

DIRECTIONS

From the intersection of the CA 405 and CA 133 freeways: Take CA 133 (Laguna Canyon Road) south toward Laguna Beach. Go 5.3 miles. The entrance to the parking lot is on the right, 0.25 miles past the stoplight at El Toro Rd.

From the intersection of Pacific Coast Highway and CA 133: Take Broadway Avenue and continue straight as it becomes CA 133 (Laguna Canyon Road). The entrance to the parking lot is on the left, after 3.3 miles.

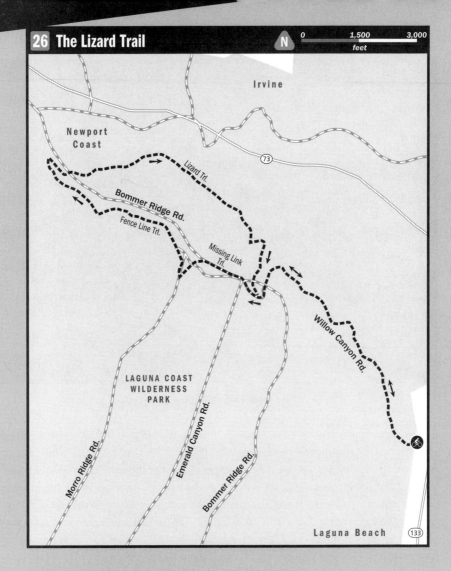

Irvine

Newport
Coast

73

Lizard Trl.

Bommer Ridge Rd.

Fence Line Trl.

Missing Link
Trl.

Willow Canyon Rd.

LAGUNA COAST
WILDERNESS
PARK

Morro Ridge Rd.

Emerald Canyon Rd.

Bommer Ridge Rd.

Laguna Beach

133

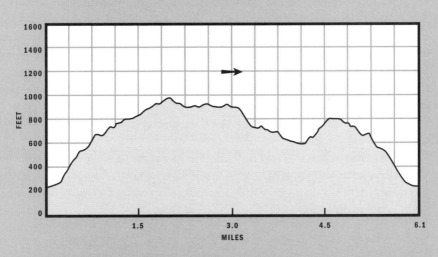

1600
1400
1200
1000
800
600
400
200
0

FEET

1.5   3.0   4.5   6.1
MILES

The trailhead at Willow Canyon

cluster of sycamores and live oaks. However, the flat, shaded section is short-lived: after 300 yards the road leaves the trees and turns steeply uphill. The most difficult climbing comes first—steep, challenging sections of road are graded out of the boulder-strewn ridgeline. In a short time you are looking down 400 feet to the canyon. After 0.8 miles the incline decreases and the road turns smooth. Strong climbers may be able to do the rest of the climb in the middle chainring. The route here is cut into the eastern side of the ridge, allowing for views of Laurel Canyon below. Although it looks tempting, bicycles are not permitted in the lower section of Laurel Canyon, so don't think about riding there.

After 1.4 miles there are two, nearly adjacent forks in the road. Continue straight at the first fork and veer right at the second fork. Climb up this road to the gate where El Morro Ridge Road ends. At 1.9 miles pass through the gate to Crystal Cove State Park and follow the road for 150 yards. Turn right on a well-worn dirt path; it's a short ride up to Photoman Point. At 1,007 feet, Photoman is the highest point in Crystal Cove and just a few feet lower than Top of the World, the highest point in Laguna. This, of course, means the climb is complete. Allow a moment or two to take in the panoramic view of the Laguna Coast Wilderness. Perhaps you can imagine (or even remember) how it appeared before they built the toll road.

Before heading down, it may be prudent to survey the Missing Link Trail for traffic. The trail runs fast with plenty of tight turns and dips. However, there are also several blind spots. Avoid surprise encounters with other hikers and bikers; be careful and, when in doubt, make plenty of noise.

At 2.6 miles Missing Link Trail ends at West Loop Road. Cross the road and continue on the Fence Line Trail. This singletrack runs flatter and smoother than Missing Link Trail, but still offers plenty of tight corners. Crank hard and use momentum to carry yourself to Red Tail Ridge. Turn right here and head down 50 feet to a gate. Here, 3 miles into the ride, turn right at Bommer Ridge Road and keep your eyes open. Before you make 3.2 miles, the Lizard Trail heads left. An old rusty irrigation pipe crosses the path at the junction.

Head down the Lizard Trail. The drop isn't steep, but you encounter a variety of surface conditions—dips, ruts, off-camber sections, and rock faces. This is a good place to improve your bike-handling skills. In short time, you wind into the upper end of Laurel Canyon. From here the path twists and weaves under a dense cover of foliage, heading imperceptibly downhill. The trail tends to be overgrown, and there are plenty of low branches, so eye protection and gloves are a necessity. Some may even want to wear long sleeves.

The Lizard Trail may not offer adrenaline-charged riding, but it is fun and invigorating. You'll be tempted to take a moment and enjoy the serene and tranquil confines of the canyon, easily forgetting that the CA 73 freeway looms nearby. At 3.8 miles the trail climbs around and over some minivan-sized boulders. Only those with serious trials skills will be able to ride this section, but it is easily hiked. Past the boulders the trail drops into an open meadow and winds through head-high brush for another 0.4 miles.

At 4.3 miles the Lizard Trail dead-ends at an unnamed fire road. Head right and climb back to the ridge. The climb is quick and painless, a small price to pay for more than 2 miles of fun singletrack riding. Just past 4.7 miles you reach Willow Canyon Road, where you head left and downhill.

The final descent retraces the initial climb, a nice payback for the initial uphill grind. The road runs fast and smooth with wide-open turns. However, be mindful of other bikers and also hikers, particularly on a couple of blind turns midway down the hill.

After the Ride

Since you've conquered the Lizard Trail, you may want to give Wahoo's tacos a try. Wahoo's, an Orange County institution, was originally modeled after the taco stands of Baja California. Today the menu offers a great selection of tasty, filling, and nicely priced meals. The Laguna location is on Pacific Coast Highway about a mile south of Main Beach.

Wahoo's Laguna Beach
1133 Pacific Coast Highway
Laguna Beach, CA 92651
(949) 497-0033

27

ALTA LAGUNA TRAINING RIDE

KEY AT-A-GLANCE INFORMATION

Length: 5.1 miles

Configuration: Loop

Aerobic difficulty: Moderate to difficult; one grueling climb

Technical difficulty: Relatively easy; the dirt section is all on fire roads.

Exposure: Complete sun

Scenery: Famed Laguna Beach ocean views

Trail traffic: Light to moderate

Riding time: 40 minutes–1 hour

Access: Free street parking is available near Laguna Beach High School. In summer, when street space is at a premium, Laguna Beach offers free parking in the school-district lot across from the high school.

Special comments: The start and end point for this ride is somewhat arbitrary. I chose the high school since it is a recognizable landmark and parking is much less of a hassle than in nearby downtown Laguna.

In Brief

This is a short and fast loop, but the 1,000 feet of climbing is enough to make your legs burn. The climb, following paved roads, begins at Laguna Beach High School and heads straight up to Top of the World. It's no wonder they call it Top of the World—it's the highest point in Laguna, and the views are stunning. After the climb, a short ride on Alta Laguna Boulevard leads to Alta Laguna Park. From here, several routes lead to Laguna Canyon, and some are extremely steep and technical. This loop takes the quickest and easiest route, a winding fire-road descent to Canyon Acres. From the gate at Canyon Acres, a quick coast through the neighborhood takes you to Laguna Canyon Road. From there it is a short ride to Third Street in downtown Laguna. The climb up Third Street provides one last test before you arrive back at the high school. Short and sweet, with a good deal of sweat.

Description

Ride uphill on Park Avenue past the high school and tennis courts. After 0.2 miles turn left at a stop sign onto Skyline Drive. The climb starts steep and remains steep, rising 550 feet in 0.9 miles. At 1.1 miles the road levels, the beginning of a short respite before the last chunk of the climb. Turn right on Caribbean Way at 1.5 miles, coast down, and then head immediately left on Tahiti Avenue.

GPS TRAILHEAD COORDINATES (WGS 84)
UTM Zone (WGS84) 11S
Easting 0427783
Northing 3711657
Latitude N 33°32'32"
Longitude W 117°46'40"

DIRECTIONS

From the intersection of the CA 405 and CA 133 freeways: Take CA 133 (Laguna Canyon Road) south. Follow the canyon road 7.8 miles to Laguna Beach. Turn left on Forest Avenue. After 0.1 mile head straight onto Third Street. Follow Third Street up a big hill and then turn immediately left on Park Avenue. The school-district parking lot is on the left, just past Blumont Street. If the lot is closed, street parking is available on Blumont Street and also on Short Street.

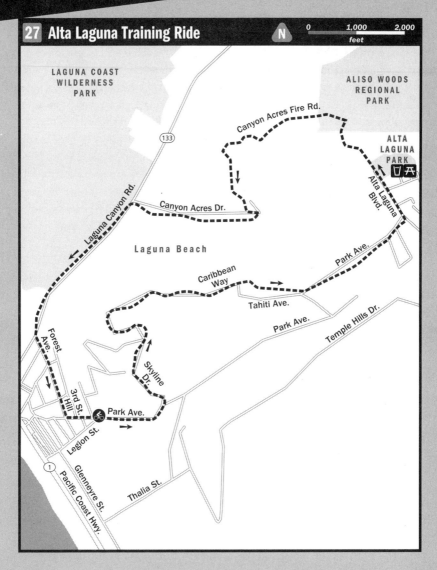

N
0   1,000   2,000
feet

LAGUNA COAST
WILDERNESS
PARK

ALISO WOODS
REGIONAL
PARK

Canyon Acres Fire Rd.

ALTA
LAGUNA
PARK

133

Alta Laguna Blvd.

Canyon Acres Dr.

Laguna Canyon Rd.

Laguna Beach

Park Ave.

Caribbean Way

Tahiti Ave.

Park Ave.

Temple Hills Dr.

Forest Ave.

Skyline Dr.

3rd St.

Hill

Park Ave.

Legion St.

1

Glenneyre St.

Pacific Coast Hwy.

Thalia St.

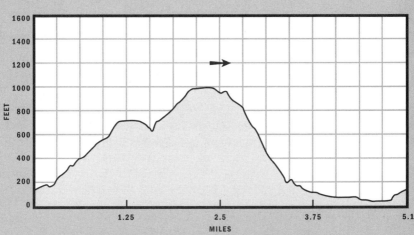

FEET
1600
1400
1200
1000
800
600
400
200
0

1.25   2.5   3.75   5.1
MILES

The road continues downhill a bit, unfortunately losing about 80 feet of hard-fought eleva-tion gain, and eventually brings you back to Park Avenue. Continue uphill on Park Avenue. It is a straight grind to Alta Laguna Boulevard: 300 feet of elevation gain in 0.5 miles. There is a significant amount of traffic on Park Avenue, particularly on weekends. Fortunately, the upper section is much wider, and more bicycle friendly, than the lower section.

The top of the hill is always in clear view throughout the last section of the climb, but it doesn't arrive fast. As your legs begin to burn, you might be inclined to wonder why pro cyclists consider using performance-enhancing drugs. Finally, at 2.2 miles, the climb ends at Top of the World. Life is good!

Head left on Alta Laguna Boulevard, following it until it dead-ends at a cul-de-sac. You'll probably see other mountain bikers unloading bikes from their vehicles; be sure to remind them that you *rode* your bike up the hill.

Alta Laguna Park lies just beyond the cul-de-sac. The amenities of the park include a pic-nic table, a water fountain, and postcard-quality views. Clear days offer unobstructed views of Catalina Island. Exceptionally clear days allow views of distant San Clemente Island. (*Note:* dogs are permitted in the upper part of the park.)

Two fire roads begin at the picnic table. The road to the right follows the ridge to Aliso Woods. Take the road on the left and head west toward Canyon Acres. At 2.5 miles a hiking trail veers left and heads toward Park Avenue. Veer right and follow the road. Soon the route turns steeply downhill, allowing for an unfettered cruise into the canyon. A number of small trails intersect the Canyon Acres road, running parallel toward the canyon. You won't get lost on any of these trails; however, while fun, they offer varying degrees of difficulty, and some options lead to steep drop-offs. At 3.2 miles the road splits: turn left to avoid an extra, unnec-essary loop. The bottom of the hill arrives quickly. Go through the gate at Canyon Acres and head down the street to a stoplight at Laguna Canyon. Go left on Laguna Canyon Road and then, at 4.7 miles, turn left on Forest Avenue. Continue straight toward the Third Street hill. This is your last challenge—a short, super-steep grind uphill. Drop down into an easy gear, watch for cars, and then go for it.

Note: The climbing section of the route begins on Park Avenue, detours to Skyline Drive, and then returns to Park Avenue near the finish. Simply staying on Park Avenue results in a slightly shorter and steeper climb to Top of the World. However, Park Avenue has a great deal of high-speed traffic. The generally tranquil climb up Skyline Drive offers the possibility of side-by-side riding with your buddy and, if you're lucky, some friendly homeowners may offer to cool you down with their hose.

After the Ride

Walk or ride to downtown Laguna. You will find a variety of restaurants on Forest and Ocean avenues. I recommend Zinc Café on Ocean Avenue, just across from the post office. The food is healthy, and there is always an interesting mix of people dining outdoors on the patio.

Zinc Café
350 Ocean Avenue
Laguna Beach, CA 92651
(949) 494-6302

28

TELONICS DOWNHILL

KEY AT-A-GLANCE INFORMATION

Length: 1 mile

Configuration: Shuttle ride

Aerobic difficulty: None to moderate; depending if you climb back up the hill

Technical difficulty: Difficult to extreme; steep, rocky, and hairy

Exposure: Mostly complete sun

Scenery: Keep your eyes on the trail

Trail traffic: Moderate

Riding time: 2–10 minutes

Access: Free parking is available near the top of the trail on Alta Laguna Drive. Free parking and metered parking are available near the bottom of the trail on Laguna Canyon Road.

Special comments: Use extreme caution to avoid injuring yourself and others. The trail is somewhat stressed from overuse. Do not ride Telonics when it is wet or muddy.

In Brief

Telonics is a steep, technical downhill that begins at Top of the World and plummets to Laguna Canyon. You'll need suspension, guts, skills, and perhaps a bit of body armor to make the trip. Start near the picnic tables at Alta Laguna Park and follow the singletrack that parallels, crosses, and finally veers away from the Canyon Acres fire road. The trail ends near the big bend in Laguna Canyon Road, right next to the Telonics building.

Description

This trail has as much history as any trail in Orange County. Telonics was the sight of one of the first downhill races in the country—The Leaping Lizard Freefall. It also provided the downhill section to the annual Rad Challenge. The first time I ever rode down the trail, on a 24-inch Panasonic mountain bike with no suspension, I did cartwheels into the bushes. It took me two years to get the courage to ride it again. Perhaps every local mountain biker has a story or two about the trail. GT shot promotional photos here. Timothy Leary got arrested here. Who knows what else?

Today, with the advent of extreme downhill bikes, the trail is more popular than ever, and it looks a bit worse from the wear. Local riders were perturbed when Brian

GPS TRAILHEAD COORDINATES (WGS 84)

UTM Zone (WGS84) 11S
Easting 0429420
Northing 3713215
Latitude N 33°33'23"
Longitude W 117°45'37"

DIRECTIONS

From the intersection of the CA 405 and CA 133 freeways: Take CA 133 (Laguna Canyon Road) south toward Laguna Beach. Go 8.5 miles through the canyon. Turn left on Forest Avenue, just past the Festival of the Arts grounds. After 0.1 mile continue straight onto Third Street. Head up the steep hill and then turn left on Park Avenue. Follow Park Avenue 1.6 miles to Alta Laguna Boulevard. Turn left on Alta Laguna Boulevard, continue 0.3 miles to a cul-de-sac, and park.

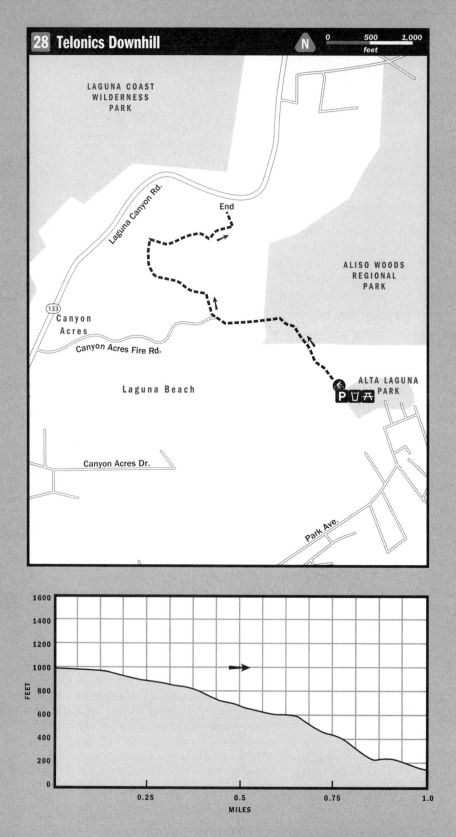

N

0   500   1,000
feet

LAGUNA COAST
WILDERNESS
PARK

Laguna Canyon Rd.

End

ALISO WOODS
REGIONAL
PARK

133

Canyon
Acres

Canyon Acres Fire Rd.

Laguna Beach

ALTA LAGUNA
PARK

P

Canyon Acres Dr.

Park Ave.

Lopes spoke on the Outdoor Life Network about car shuttling to the top of Laguna and riding downhill. But today, that trend is here to stay. You can shuttle to the top of Telonics or you can do it the old way—hike up the trail and ride down. The advantage to hiking the trail is that you have some time to check the course and pick your lines.

The downhill starts just past the picnic tables at Alta Laguna Park. Fork immediately left onto the Canyon Acres fire road. Fifty yards ahead, where the road turns slightly downhill, veer right onto the upper section of the trail. The singletrack winds around the top of the hillside before crossing and then merging with the Canyon Acres fire road. Head briefly down toward Canyon Acres, and then, near 0.4 miles, turn right onto the Telonics Trail. This is where the fun begins. The path plummets down a steep hillside and then drops left through a steep rock course. Continue straight over a series of slick rocks. This is a good spot to stop and check the view. Look straight down on the big bend. It almost feels like you're suspended directly over the canyon floor.

Past the rocks, the trail narrows and snakes north. After a left turn you'll hit the Tank Trap—a steep rutted incline with interspersed rock ledges. There are three lines down this section. The middle line is the most direct but has the biggest drop-off. If you make it past the Tank Trap, there's just one more difficult section. Turn right and head under a canopy of live oaks. Past the trees is the last steep and rutted drop. Stay on your back wheel and keep enough speed so you don't spin out. That's all it takes—momentum, confidence, and a bit of skill.

The final leg of the trail runs through (very unofficial) Timothy Leary Park and ends at the Telonics parking lot. The best times in the Leaping Lizard Freefall tended to be around two minutes. Give yourself a few practice runs before you try to meet that standard.

After the Ride
If you don't need to go to the walk-in clinic, head to the Marine Room in downtown Laguna. You can celebrate your successful Telonics run and toss back a couple of frosty mugs of beer. Just don't try to regale the bartenders with your mountain bike exploits—they won't listen.

Marine Room
214 Ocean Avenue
Laguna Beach, CA 92651
(949) 494-3027

ALISO AND WOOD CANYONS

WOOD CANYON LOOP

KEY AT-A-GLANCE INFORMATION

Length: 10.3 miles

Configuration: Loop with 4-mile out-and-back (2 miles each way)

Aerobic difficulty: Fairly easy; the only real heart pumping comes on the Cholla Trail, and it's short-lived.

Technical difficulty: Moderate with fun but not technical singletrack

Exposure: Complete sun in Aliso Canyon but plenty of shady sections in Wood Canyon

Scenery: Wood Canyon might have the greatest density of indigenous trees of anywhere in coastal Orange County

Trail traffic: Light on weekdays and moderately crowded on weekends

Riding time: 1–1.5 hours

Access: Enter Aliso and Wood Canyons Wilderness Park from Alicia Parkway. Plenty of parking is available in the dirt lot. You will need 3 somewhat crisp dollar bills for the automated parking machine. Additional parking is available on the nearby streets; it's free but limited.

GPS TRAILHEAD COORDINATES (WGS 84)
UTM Zone (WGS84) 11S
Easting 0433146
Northing 3712697
Latitude N 33°33'07"
Longitude W 117°43'13"

In Brief

This loop has a very narrow configuration, heading up Wood Canyon on the Wood Canyon Trail and returning on a few fun, easily managed singletracks. Spin 1.5 miles down Aliso Canyon to access Wood Canyon. A fairly mellow ride up the canyon precedes a short burst up the Cholla Trail to the ridgeline. This is where the fun begins. Follow the ridge to the Lynx Trail and charge back into the canyon. Retrace the canyon a short distance to the Coyote Run Trail and then crank all the way to the Mathis Trail. From Mathis, a short and scenic diversion on the Dripping Cave Trail brings you back to Wood Canyon. The ride's last 2 miles retrace the first 2.

Information

Aliso and Wood Canyons Wilderness Park
28373 Alicia Parkway
Laguna Niguel, CA 92677
(949) 923-2200

Description

This ride offers a fine payoff for the amount of effort expended. The lone true climb, steep but short-lived, precedes a lengthy run on two fun sections of singletrack. So you may want to consider this route when you're out of shape but still pining for a necessary adrenaline rush.

DIRECTIONS

From central and northern Orange County: Take the CA 405 freeway south to where it merges with the CA 5 freeway. Continue another 3.2 miles, now on CA 5, and exit at Alicia Parkway. Turn right and go 3.9 miles. Just past the intersection with Aliso Creek Road, turn right on Awma Road. The park entrance is on the left.

From Pacific Coast Highway: Take Crown Valley Parkway 2.9 miles to Alicia Parkway. Turn left and go 2.1 miles to Awma Road. Turn left on Awma Road. The park entrance is on the left.

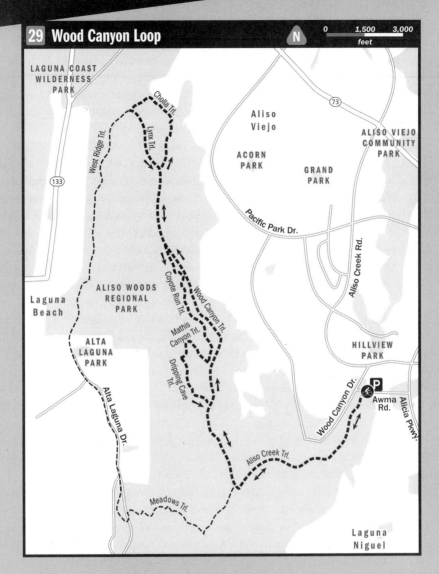

0   1,500   3,000
feet

N

LAGUNA COAST
WILDERNESS
PARK

Cholla Trl.

Lynx Trl.

West Ridge Trl.

133

Aliso
Viejo

73

ACORN
PARK

GRAND
PARK

ALISO VIEJO
COMMUNITY
PARK

Pacific Park Dr.

Aliso Creek Rd.

Laguna
Beach

ALISO WOODS
REGIONAL
PARK

Coyote Run Trl.

Wood Canyon Trl.

Mathis
Canyon Trl.

Dripping Cave
Trl.

ALTA
LAGUNA
PARK

Alta Laguna Dr.

HILLVIEW
PARK

Wood Canyon Dr.

P

Awma
Rd.

Alicia Pkwy.

Aliso Creek Trl.

Meadows Trl.

Laguna
Niguel

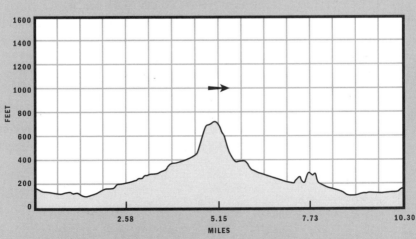

Beginning in Aliso Canyon, the first section is easy and uneventful. Near the start, the Aliso Creek Trail is nothing more than a dirt shoulder for the paved county access road. After 0.3 miles the trail veers away from the road but runs parallel to it. You have the option of riding on the road, but why would you? The Aliso Creek Trail ends at the bottom of Wood Canyon. The paved road continues down Aliso Canyon, but it's not open to the public.

Near 1.5 miles turn up the Wood Canyon Trail, a dirt road. Almost immediately you'll pass a series of slick-rock formations that look tempting to climb. If you are so inclined, the rocks are accessible by a few hiking trails. Continuing up the canyon, the dirt road runs wide and smooth, climbing imperceptibly. The road crosses Wood Creek three times: concrete culverts and minimal water flow make for easy passages. The last crossing has the option of a wooden footbridge. Past 3 miles the trees grow thicker and eventually form a dense canopy. Here the canyon narrows and the grade increases, though the climb is easily managed.

At 4.5 miles a kiosk designates the start of the Cholla Trail. This is the only taxing climb of the ride. The steep singletrack has widely arced switchbacks. Most of the trail is smooth and easily cleaned. Crank hard—you'll be at the top before you know it.

At the top of the Cholla Trail, turn left on the ridgeline. At 5 miles turn left again on the Lynx Trail and begin your descent. Lynx Trail is a bit ruttier and rockier than the Cholla Trail, but it's fun and not too technical. Near 5.6 miles the Lynx Trail rejoins the Wood Canyon Trail. Head right and crank back through the trees, keeping an eye out for the Coyote Run Trail.

Near 6.1 miles veer right on Coyote Run Trail. The singletrack runs parallel to Wood Canyon Trail, dipping and winding along the tree-lined creek. It's not steep, so you'll have to push a bit to take full advantage of the course. Be mindful of other trail users: you don't want a surprise encounter on one of the blind turns. A short, steep climb comes unexpectedly near the 7-mile point—you'll have to be in a fairly low gear to make the grade. Past the steep rise the trail drops down to the Mathis Canyon Trail.

Turn right onto the Mathis Canyon Trail. Before the trail begins to climb to West Ridge, veer left on the Dripping Cave Trail. This trail gains about 80 feet of elevation, climbing through a grove of live oaks and switchbacking up to a narrow ridge. A short, easy descent now drops into a densely foliated grotto. Near 8 miles a small footpath leads to the Dripping Cave—a wavelike sandstone wash that's been carved over the years by flowing water. This is a nice spot to put your bike down and explore, but stay on the trail to avoid poison oak.

Past the cave a short spin leads back to the Wood Canyon Trail. Turn right and head back toward Aliso Canyon. Then, at 8.8 miles, turn left on the Aliso Creek Trail and spin the last 1.5 miles back to the parking lot.

After the Ride

Follow nearby Aliso Canyon Road into the perfectly planned community of Aliso Viejo. About a mile up from Alicia Parkway, you'll find Pacific Park Plaza—a strip mall with pedestrian fast food and boring chain stores. Luckily, they put a Z Pizza in the mall as well. Be thankful.

Z Pizza
26921 Aliso Creek Road
Aliso Viejo, CA 92656
(949) 425-0102

30

MEADOWS TRAIL LOOP

GPS TRAILHEAD COORDINATES (WGS 84)

UTM Zone (WGS84) 11S
Easting 0433146
Northing 3712697
Latitude N 33°33'07"
Longitude W 117°43'13"

In Brief

This ride nearly circumnavigates the Aliso and Wood Canyon Wilderness Area, offering a bit of everything: dirt roads, singletrack, hike-a-bike, and even a bit of road riding. Begin on the Aliso Creek Trail and then continue on the Wood Canyon Trail. After the lengthy warm-up, a short hike-a-bike on the Lynx Trail leads to the West Ridge Trail. Crank uphill on the West Ridge Trail to the park's upper entrance at Alta Laguna Drive. Exit the park onto Alta Laguna Drive and follow the paved road until it ends. A short traverse on singletrack puts you on a paved fire road that leads to the Meadows Trail. The Meadows Trail switchbacks all the way back down to Aliso Canyon. The last 1.5 miles retrace the initial ride on the Aliso Creek Trail.

Information

Aliso and Wood Canyons Wilderness Park
28373 Alicia Parkway
Laguna Niguel, CA 92677
(949) 923-2200

Description

Aliso and Wood Canyons Park threads its way between Laguna Canyon, Alta Laguna, Aliso Viejo, and Laguna

DIRECTIONS

From central and northern Orange County: Take CA 405 freeway south to where it merges with CA 5 freeway. Continue another 3.2 miles, now on CA 5, and exit at Alicia Parkway. Turn right and go 3.9 miles. Just past the intersection with Aliso Creek Road, turn left on Awma Road. The park entrance is on the left.

From Pacific Coast Highway: Take Crown Valley Parkway 2.9 miles to Alicia Parkway. Turn left and go 2.1 miles to Awma Road. Turn left on Awma Road. The park entrance is on the left.

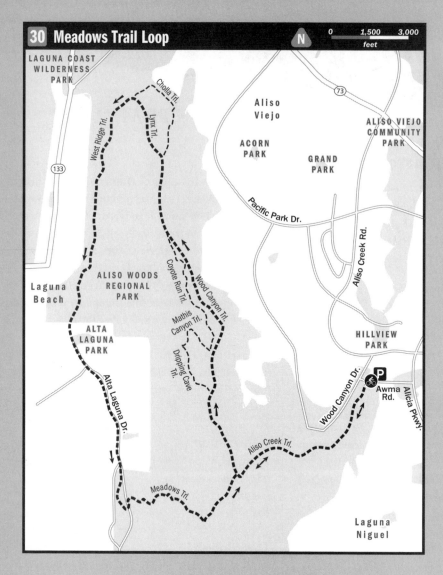

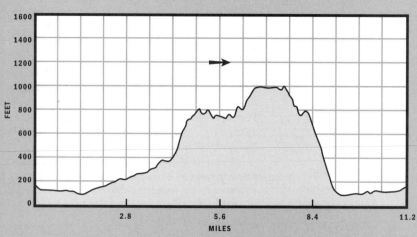

Niguel. The park may be accessed from several points along its boundaries, although the most popular (and accessible) entrances are at Alta Laguna and Alicia Parkway. One of the advantages of entering from Alicia Parkway is the amount of warm-up time afforded to you before having to climb. Anyone familiar with riding in Laguna Beach knows that the terrain tends to head quickly uphill. This ride, utilizing the flat basin of Aliso Creek, has 4 miles of relatively level riding before the major climbing begins.

Begin on the Aliso Creek Trail; the path runs parallel to a paved county access road. You may ride on the paved road, but the trail provides better conditioning (at least mentally) and is generally less crowded. After 1.5 miles veer away from the pavement onto the Wood Canyon Trail (a dirt road). This is where the backcountry begins in earnest. Wood Canyon, much narrower than Aliso Canyon, is dotted with rock formations, mature trees, and wildlife. There is also plenty of good mountain biking here—every singletrack in the park connects to Wood Canyon.

The route continues to be relatively flat even as the canyon narrows. At 2.2 miles the Mathis Canyon Trail climbs left. Here you may also access the Coyote Run Trail—a winding singletrack that runs parallel to the Wood Canyon Trail. Diverting onto the Coyote Run Trail is a viable option for this ride. The only caveat is that most cyclists ride Coyote Run Trail in the opposite direction, and you may be constantly running against traffic on the trail.

Continue spinning toward the upper reaches of Wood Canyon. The Wood Canyon Trail winds through a grove of sycamores and begins to climb alongside upper Wood Creek. These first grades are gentle and shady, almost not worth mentioning. At 4.1 miles follow the Lynx Trail out from under the canopy of trees, heading up a narrow and scenic arroyo to the ridgeline. The trail—steep, rutted, and rocky—will require you to dismount and hike-a-bike some sections. (If you have a political, cultural, or religious opposition to the practice of hike-a-biking, you may ride the Cholla Trail to the ridgeline; this option will add 1 mile to the loop. To get to the Cholla Trail, continue on the Wood Canyon Trail 0.5 miles past the Lynx Trail.)

At 5 miles the Lynx Trail connects to the West Ridge Trail (a dirt road); here head left and follow the ridgeline. Laguna Canyon is below and to the right as the road rolls and climbs to Alta Laguna. As you grind along the ridge, you will pass markers designating the Rock-It and Mathis Canyon trails, two drops into Wood Canyon. Other unmarked trails head into Laguna Canyon, including Stair Steps, which drops down near the water tower. The final climb on the West Ridge Trail, the longest and the steepest of this route, brings you to the picnic tables at Alta Laguna Park—the apex of the ride. This is a great place to stop, catch your breath, and take in the panoramic view.

From the picnic tables head left (southeast), exiting the park onto the pavement in the Top of the World neighborhood. Cruise along Alta Laguna Drive through a quiet residential area. Continue straight past Park Avenue, staying on Alta Laguna Drive almost until it ends. Near 7.5 miles look for a wooden sign reading OLD TOP OF THE WORLD. Past the sign, head right on the *second* dirt path. This is the only legal way to access the next part of the ride, since a property line keeps the Moulton Meadows fire road from reaching Alta Laguna Drive. Skirting around a property line, drop down the rugged trail, then hike-a-bike a short

The view from atop the Meadows Trail

distance to a paved fire road. This road runs along the saddle above Aliso Canyon. Below, to the west, is Bluebird Canyon, the site where a major landslide destroyed several homes in 2004. The wreckage has been cleaned up, but signs of the slide still remain.

At 8.1 miles a kiosk marks the top of the Meadows Trail—the only way to go is down. The trail drops 700 feet in a quick mile, coursing around wide, user-friendly switchbacks. The only deterrent is the recurrent, teeth-rattling washboard. Just hope you have some decent suspension and a good dental plan. Eventually the trail flattens onto the relatively wide plain of Aliso Canyon. Near 9.2 miles veer left across a wooden bridge. The last 0.4 miles of the Meadows Trail run parallel and above a paved county access road. This part of the road isn't open to the public, so stay on the trail.

The Meadows Trail ends near the base of the Wood Canyon Trail. Turn right and then head immediately left on the Aliso Creek Trail. And that's it—the last 1.5 miles of the route retraces the beginning of the ride. It's a quick and easy push back to the parking lot.

31

ROCK-IT\LOOP

Length: 6.3 miles

Configuration: Loop with 1.2-mile out-and-back (0.6 miles each way)

Aerobic difficulty: One steep climb (800 feet of elevation gain) comes at the end of the ride.

Technical difficulty: Not too difficult; the Rock-It Trail has, go figure, plenty of rocks, but they are easier to ride than they appear.

Exposure: Complete sun, except for a few patches of trees in the canyon

Scenery: Ocean and canyon views, caves and rock formations, canopies of live oaks

Trail traffic: Light to moderate; most traffic snarls occur near the trailhead and on the Coyote Run Trail.

Riding time: 1–1.5 hours

Access: Free parking is available near the trailhead on Alta Laguna Drive. The ride cuts through Laguna and Wood Canyon Wilderness Park. The park is open daily, 7 a.m.–sunset, but is closed following rain.

GPS TRAILHEAD COORDINATES (WGS 84)

UTM Zone (WGS84) 11S
Easting 0429425
Northing 3713204
Latitude N 33°33'22"
Longitude W 117°45'37"

In Brief

The trailhead at Alta Laguna Boulevard represents the highest elevation on the route. This means that all the climbing comes at the end of the ride. The initial downhill to Wood Canyon begins on West Ridge Road and finishes with a rambunctiously bumpy ride down the Rock-It Trail. The fun continues as you wind out of the Coyote Run Trail to Mathis Canyon. A short, scenic detour along the Dripping Cave Trail loops back to the Mathis Canyon Trail. This is where you have to make up all the lost elevation. The Mathis Canyon Trail is a brute of a climb, but it's the fastest way back up to the ridge. From the top of the Mathis Canyon Trail, backtrack along West Ridge Road, up one steep climb, to the trailhead.

Information

Aliso and Wood Canyons Wilderness Park
28373 Alicia Parkway
Laguna Niguel, CA 92677
(949) 923-2200

Description

From the picnic tables follow West Ridge Road to the right (inland). The road runs straight and grows to about freeway width as it heads almost immediately downhill.

DIRECTIONS

From the intersection of the CA 405 and CA 133 freeways: take CA 133 (Laguna Canyon Road) south toward Laguna Beach. Go 8.5 miles through the canyon. Turn left on Forest Avenue, just past the Festival of the Arts grounds. After 0.1 mile continue straight onto Third Street. Head up the steep hill and then turn left on Park Avenue. Follow Park Avenue 1.6 miles to Alta Laguna Boulevard. Turn left on Alta Laguna Boulevard, continue 0.3 miles to a cul-de-sac, and park.

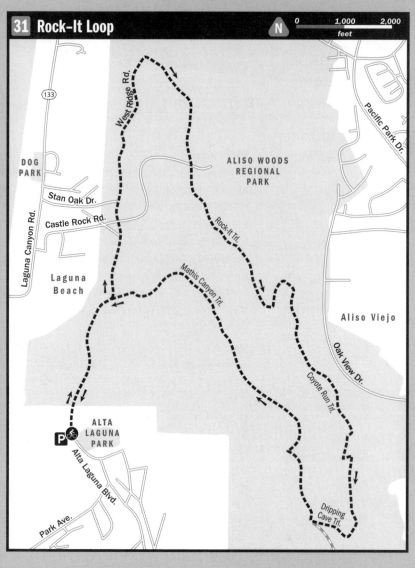

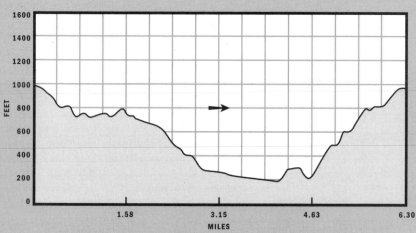

A fair number of hikers and dog walkers use the road, so give them space—there's plenty of room for everyone. After reaching maximum velocity on the downhill, use momentum to carry you through a sequence of rolling climbs and drops. After a couple of short climbs, look for a round concrete reservoir. About 100 yards before the reservoir, at 1.5 miles, the Rock-It Trail begins on the right side of the road. It is easy to see the trail, but the marker is small and difficult to read.

The Rock-It Trail quickly narrows to a singletrack, winding through the brush along a thin ridge. Initially the trail runs fairly level. Crank through the turns—the top section is fast and smooth. At 2 miles, where the trail begins to drop steadily, you'll encounter the rock sections, smatterings of appliance-sized boulders. Generally the rocks are easy to ride, more exhilarating than stressful. Just keep your momentum, bouncing along, using your suspension to full advantage. The most technical part of the trail, actually a climb, comes near the 2.5-mile point. The last section of the trail is relatively smooth and wide open, ending in Wood Canyon.

At the bottom of the trail, near 2.8 miles, head right on the Coyote Run Trail. This is a fun extension to the downhill. The Coyote Run Trail cascades in and out of trees along Wood Creek. Crank hard for maximum effect, but be mindful of other riders and hikers. A handlebar bell is not a bad idea.

Near 3.6 miles the Coyote Run Trail ends at the Mathis Canyon Trail. Rather than commit to climbing immediately, enjoy a bit more of the canyon. Head left on the Mathis Canyon Trail and then almost immediately right on the Wood Canyon Trail. At 4 miles turn right on the Dripping Cave Trail. Head through the trees to the cave. This is a great place to stop and explore, have lunch, or just try and forget about the climb ahead.

Past the cave, the trail climbs briefly but then switchbacks downward, dropping beneath a cluster of live oaks. At 4.6 miles turn left on the Mathis Canyon Trail—within 100 yards you'll be grinding straight uphill. The path is steep, but it's wide and smooth, so if you have the legs, you can make the entire climb. Near the 5.3-mile point you'll pass through a gate. Don't get your hopes up, because there is plenty more climbing to come. Finally, at 5.7 miles, the Mathis Canyon Trail ends at West Ridge Road. Head left on the ridge and make the last climb back to the picnic tables. As you're grinding up the last section of road, pay no attention to the other bikers whizzing downhill: you've already had your fun.

Note: Alta Laguna Park offers an alternative entrance to Aliso and Wood Canyons Park. Certainly many things make Alta Laguna an attractive access point: free and plentiful parking, smaller crowds, great post-ride views, and a shorter drive (than Alicia Parkway) if you're coming from most of the coastal cities in Orange County. The drawback is that all the rides from Alta Laguna Drive run downhill first and finish with a climb. This is sacrilegious to those who want to get the hard work of the climb done first and then revel in the joys of the downhill. There are options to get around this problem, but they all involve more climbing. This ride may be paired with a climb up Skyline Drive (see Ride 27, Alta Laguna Training Ride, page 120) and a drop into Laguna Canyon via the Canyon Acres fire road or the steep and technical Telonics Trail. You may also begin in Laguna Canyon (see the access notes on The Lizard Trail for parking instructions, page 116), but climbs from the canyon to Alta Laguna are steep and will probably involve hiking.

A few bread box–sized boulders on Rock-It

After the Ride

Head down the hill and go north on Pacific Coast Highway. Just up the hill from Main Beach (and next to the Cottage Restaurant), look for Madison Square and Garden Café. The food is tasty and the seating is outside in the shady and comfortable garden—perfect when you're sweaty and dirty. The restaurant is also dog friendly. Watch for the owner; he loves to fawn over his customer's pampered canines.

Madison Square and Garden Café

320 North Coast Highway

Laguna Beach, CA 92651

(949) 494-0137

TRABUCO CREEK-
SADDLEBACK VALLEY

32

ARROYO TRABUCO

Length: 15 miles

Configuration: Out-and-back

Aerobic difficulty: Moderate; no extended climbs, just 15 miles of spinning

Technical difficulty: Easy to moderate; the stream crossings are the only challenge.

Exposure: Plenty of shade

Scenery: Native riparian vegetation, streams, and graffiti-free underpasses

Trail traffic: Light

Riding time: 1.25–2 hours

Access: Free parking is available at Cox Sports Park in Ladera Ranch. Most of the ride takes place in the Arroyo Trabuco portion of O'Neill Regional Park. The upper end of the trail (the turnaround point for this ride) may be accessed from O'Neill Regional Park. Parking at all Orange County regional parks is $3 weekdays and $5 weekends.

In Brief

Begin on the footpath near the sports park, then drop down to Trabuco Canyon Road and head toward the Santa Ana Mountains. Past the Oso Parkway underpass, Trabuco Canyon Road becomes the Arroyo Trabuco Trail. This is where the stream crossings begin. Crank up the dirt trail, following the narrow, yet enticing, wilderness corridor all the way to the turnaround point at O'Neill Regional Park. The ride back is slightly downhill—fast and easy.

Information

Cox Sports Park
27701 Crown Valley Parkway
Ladera Ranch, CA 92694
(949) 584-2414

O'Neill Regional Park
30892 Trabuco Canyon Road
Trabuco Canyon, CA 92678
(949) 923-2260 or (949) 923-2256

Description

The Arroyo Trabuco Wilderness seems typical of many Orange County open-space areas—a corridor of riparian wilderness knifing between several housing developments. However, much of the recessed river bottom feels isolated from its suburban surroundings. There is also

GPS TRAILHEAD COORDINATES (WGS 84)
UTM Zone (WGS84) 11S
Easting 0439807
Northing 3714039
Latitude N 33°33'52"
Longitude W 117°38'55"

DIRECTIONS

From the intersection of the CA 405 and CA 133 freeways: Take CA 405 south toward San Diego. After 2 miles the 405 merges with the CA 5 freeway. Follow CA 5 south another 7 miles and exit at Crown Valley Parkway. Turn left on Crown Valley Parkway and go 1.5 miles, turning left into Cox Sports Park just after you cross over the Trabuco River. Park immediately on the left.

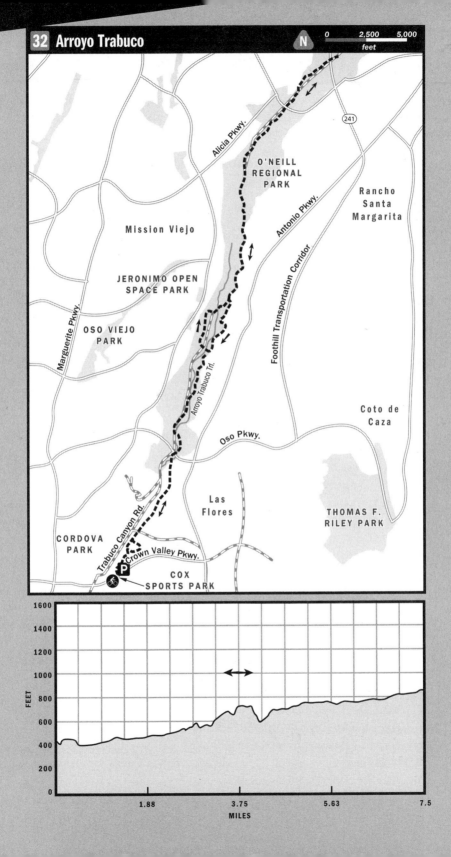

One in a series

quite a bit of water in the park. Stream crossings abound on this ride. Not just puddle hops, but full-bore "I've got to keep my speed up or I'm going to get really wet" stream crossings. It's the steeplechase of Orange County mountain biking—pure fun and a great antidote for the malaise of maturity and adulthood.

Head north (away from Crown Valley Parkway) on the footpath that parallels Cox Sports Park. After 0.35 miles turn left and downhill on an unnamed road, then quickly veer right on a singletrack that drops down to Trabuco Canyon Road. Turn right on the gravel road and start cranking. The road, unimpressive yet serviceable, runs imperceptibly uphill. Just before the Oso Parkway underpass, at 1.6 miles, the road drops down for the first of many stream crossings. Keep your speed and plow through the water. Just past the underpass, keep right and cross the stream again. This marks the beginning of the Arroyo Trabuco Trail. The dirt road follows an easy, yet surprisingly scenic, path through the tree-lined stream bottom. Don't be surprised to see deer and coyotes lurking in the narrow wilderness corridor.

The road splits near 2.4 miles. Stay left; the right fork heads to the Tijeras Creek Trail. Past 2.7 miles the road crosses the stream once more and narrows to a singletrack. Follow the vine-covered path, making tight turns beneath a canopy of junglelike foliage.

Eventually the trail widens again to a dirt road. At 3.1 miles turn left at a fork and charge through another stream crossing. This is the most difficult of the crossings, as a steep and gravelly embankment awaits on the far side of the waterway. Continue uphill, following a utility road and climbing about 150 feet above the stream bottom. You might as well push hard, since there aren't many climbs on the ride.

Turn right at 3.6 miles and drop back down into the trees. Cross the stream again and then make the slight climb to the east bluff of Arroyo Trabuco. Merge back onto the Arroyo Trabuco Trail at 4.3 miles and continue north. Near 5.4 miles veer left (don't go onto the pavement) and through a gate. The path drops, once again, to the level of the waterway. This is generally the rockiest and muddiest portion of the ride. It's not technical, but you may have to portage around a couple of mud bogs.

Pass under the Santa Margarita Parkway and stay right where the trail forks at 6.5 miles. Continue cranking up the trail. Just past the Foothill toll road underpass, the trail ends at O'Neill Regional Park. If necessary, water and restrooms are available in the regional park.

The return trip is fast. You can crank most of the trail in big gears. The mud bogs and stream crossings are even more satisfying at speed. You'll feel like a kid again, careening, splashing, and getting dirty. Retrace the trail, but stay left and on the bluff at 11 miles. A short, rocky descent leads back to the waterway, where you will retrace the singletrack and two more stream crossings.

Pass under Oso Parkway at 13.1 miles and continue back on Trabuco Canyon Road. Riding down the smooth gravel should give you an opportunity to shed some of the mud and dirt from your bike. Near 14.3 miles turn left on a paved pathway and make the final climb to the bluff. Turn right at the top and wind along the footpath back to the trailhead.

Note: All trails in O'Neill Regional Park are closed for two days after any measurable rainfall. There are several stream crossings on the ride. The creek runs from winter till at least midsummer (if not year round). This ride is not recommended after periods of substantial rainfall. High water levels in Trabuco Creek make for undesirable and possibly even dangerous riding conditions.

After the Ride

Clean up a bit and head to BeachFire Bar and Grill in Ladera Ranch. Enjoy a drink and some Pacific Rim, Caribbean, or California beach–inspired cuisine. The food is creative, tasty, and fairly priced. They have entertainment as well: check out the Web site at **www.beachfire.com.**

BeachFire Bar and Grill

25682 Crown Valley Parkway, Building 1

Ladera Ranch, CA 92694

(949) 542-7700

33

| TIJERAS CREEK LOOP

(i) KEY AT-A-GLANCE INFORMATION

Length: 18.7 miles

Configuration: 14.1-mile loop with 4.6-mile out-and-back (2.3 miles each way)

Aerobic difficulty: Moderate; plenty of spinning but few hills

Technical difficulty: Easy to moderate; once you've mastered the stream crossings, it's all gravy

Exposure: Sun and shade

Scenery: River-bottom wilderness with a few doses of suburbia

Trail traffic: Light

Riding time: 1.75–2.5 hours

Access: Free parking is available at Cox Sports Park in Ladera Ranch. The return route follows the Arroyo Trabuco corridor, part of O'Neill Regional Park.

Special comments: All trails in O'Neill Regional Park are closed for two days after any measurable rainfall. There are several stream crossings on the ride. The water runs from winter till at least midsummer. This ride is not recommended after periods of substantial rainfall. High water levels in Trabuco Creek make for undesirable and possibly even dangerous riding conditions.

In Brief

Spin up Arroyo Trabuco to Tijeras Creek. Turn right and follow a satisfying combination of singletrack, dirt roads, and suburban hiking trails all the way to Coto de Caza. Turn left on Plano Trabuco Road and ride down the pavement till you reach the back side of O'Neill Regional Park. The traverse through the regional park runs along groomed, one might say pedestrian, trails. You'll cross the creek bed near the campsites and then bear left on the Arroyo Trabuco Trail. The path runs gradually downhill all the way back to the trailhead; crank hard and charge through the stream crossings.

Information

Cox Sports Park
27701 Crown Valley Parkway
Ladera Ranch, CA 92694
(949) 584-2414

O'Neill Regional Park
30892 Trabuco Canyon Road
Trabuco Canyon, CA 92678
(949) 923-2260 or (949) 923-2256

Description

For many riders life can get in the way of staying in shape. It shouldn't be that way, but family obligations, work, school, dental appointments, and hangovers all seem to crop up at inopportune times. When you're out of shape,

GPS TRAILHEAD COORDINATES (WGS 84)
UTM Zone (WGS84) 11S
Easting 0439807
Northing 3714039
Latitude N 33°33'52"
Longitude W 117°38'55"

DIRECTIONS

From the intersection of the CA 405 and CA 133 freeways: Take CA 405 south toward San Diego. After 2 miles CA 405 merges with CA 5. Follow CA 5 south another 7 miles and exit at Crown Valley Parkway. Turn left on Crown Valley Parkway and go 1.5 miles, turning left into Cox Sports Park just after you cross over the Trabuco River. Park immediately on the left.

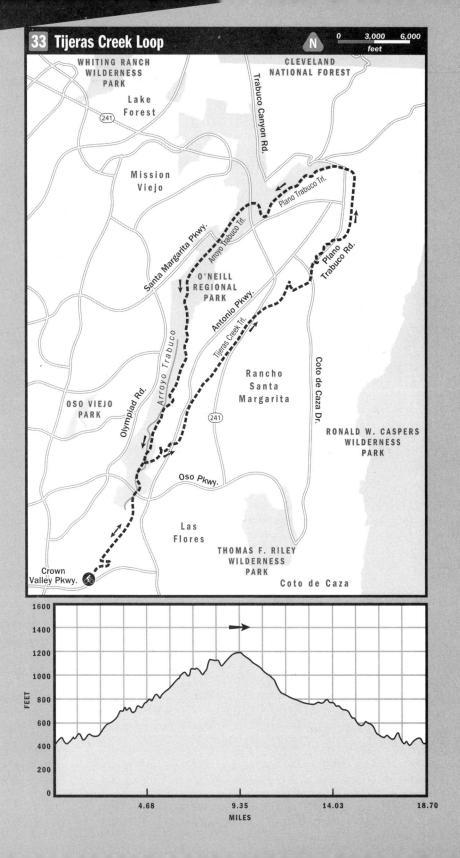

The start of the Tijeras Creek Trail

it's hard to get back in the saddle. After a spell of inactivity and a few extra pounds, it's easy to make excuses to do other activities (see hangovers, above). Perhaps the excuses are a defense mechanism against the pain of doing a grisly climb with puny lungs and extra baggage. There is a middle ground, though: long, flat rides.

The Tijeras Creek loop is a great, and mostly pain free, conditioning ride. There aren't any major hills, but a hard crank through the 19-mile course will definitely put you on the path to fitness. Luckily there are enough diversions on the route—scenery, singletrack, and stream crossings—to hold your interest. The trail isn't technically challenging, but parts of it are quite fun.

Head north (away from Crown Valley Parkway) on the footpath that parallels Cox Sports Park. After 0.35 miles turn left and downhill on an unnamed road, then quickly veer right on a singletrack that drops down to Trabuco Canyon Road. Turn right on the gravel road and start cranking. The first stream crossing comes at 1.3 miles. Splash across and then continue on the dirt, crossing under Oso Parkway. Veer right after the underpass and cross the creek again. Continue north on the Arroyo Trabuco Trail. Before long the canopy of trees completely obscures the suburban surroundings.

Turn right at 2.3 miles on the signed Tijeras Creek Trail. Plow through a broad section of the stream and then follow the singletrack through a washed-out arroyo. The trail splits at 2.7 miles, where you veer right. (The left fork leads to a makeshift tree swing: swing at your own risk.) Climb to a gate, turn left at 2.8 miles, and follow the Tijeras Creek Trail, now a dirt road, as it runs parallel and just below Antonio Parkway. Near 3.7 miles the Tijeras

Creek Trail again drops to creek level. Follow the fun and scenic singletrack all the way to an underpass beneath the CA 241 freeway. Just past the underpass, at 5.8 miles, turn away from the creek and follow the trail slightly uphill. At 5.9 miles turn right on a dirt road and continue uphill. Fork right at 6.2 miles and make a short climb to the ridgetop. At 6.6 miles turn left and crank along the rolling ridge road to Coto De Caza Drive. Continue straight across the street. This is a blind intersection, so be careful of fast moving cars.

The next section of the route follows a groomed pathway between houses and hillsides. The pathway ends near 7.9 miles at Plano Trabuco Road. Cross the street and turn left, staying on Plano Trabuco Road. Spin down the paved road as it follows an L-shaped route (OK, an upside-down L) around a walled housing development. *Do not* continue downhill on Plano Trabuco Road to Trabuco Canyon Road. Just past the perimeter of the housing complex, at 9.3 miles, cross the street, pass through a chain link fence (there is trail-width gap near the wall), and connect to a dirt path.

The dirt path leads to a paved path. Bear right, and then, at 9.6 miles, head through a gate into O'Neill Regional Park. Cross pavement and then veer left on the Plano Trabuco Trail. Ride the length of the wide, flat trail. Cruise downhill and get on pavement at 10.6 miles—there used to be a singletrack here but it is currently undergoing maintenance. At the bottom of the hill, continue straight across a gravel parking lot. Keep heading northwest and parallel to CA 241, which is about 250 yards on the left. The trail is not well defined until after you reach a rocky streambed at 11 miles. Cross the streambed, probably dry, and head straight toward a shady section of campground. Stay left of the campground. Near 11.2 miles, you'll reach a gate and the beginning of the Arroyo Trabuco Trail.

Head straight down the Arroyo Trabuco Trail toward the CA 241 underpass. It's a straight shot back to the Cox Sports Park. If you want detailed notes on this portion of the route, read the description for Ride 32, Arroyo Trabuco (page 142).

You'll pass the Tijeras Creek Trail fork at 16.4 miles, completing the loop section of the ride. Continue south, cranking through the final two stream crossings. Turn left and uphill at 18.1 miles. Atop the hill, veer right and cruise along a concrete path. Turn right at a gate, near 18.4 miles, and follow a groomed path back to the trailhead.

After the Ride

Cross Crown Valley Parkway and head to Taco Mesa. The food is improbably healthy, tasty, and authentic: you won't be disappointed. Sit on the patio and enjoy a nice view of Arroyo Trabuco.

Taco Mesa
27702 Crown Valley Parkway
Ladera Ranch, CA 92694
(949) 364-1957

34

LOWER TRABUCO CREEK LOOP

Length: 14.6 miles

Configuration: Double loop

Aerobic difficulty: Moderate; all the tough climbs come near the end.

Technical difficulty: Moderate; four makeable stream crossings and a BMX-style singletrack spice up the ride.

Exposure: Plenty of shade near the water, but complete sun on the ridges

Scenery: A plush riparian wilderness contained in suburbia. It's like Disneyland's Jungle Cruise without the plastic alligators and the cheesy narration.

Trail traffic: Mostly light

Riding time: 1.5–2.5 hours

Access: There is plenty of street parking on Trabuco Creek Road. Park where the sidewalk begins; parking is illegal near the corner of Trabuco Creek and Rancho Viejo. Also, parking is restricted on the first and third Monday mornings of the month due to street sweeping.

In Brief

Ride a short distance down Trabuco Creek Road and connect to the river bottom via a smooth dirt trail. When you reach Crown Valley Parkway, climb up to the street and follow the overpass to the Cox Sports Park. Drop down to the east side of the riparian flood plain and head up the Arroyo Trabuco Trail. Crank through three stream crossings to the Tijeras Creek Trail. Veer right on the Tijeras Creek Trail, ride a scenic section of the singletrack, and then follow a suburban multiuse path to Antonio Parkway. After a short stint on the road, drop down the Water District Trail and wind your way back to the Arroyo Trabuco Trail (completing the outer loop). Continue south along the river bottom, ride under Crown Valley Parkway, and prepare to climb. Follow the dirt road to the Trabuco ridgeline, grind through several successive steep climbs, and, eventually, drop down to Monarch Drive. Ride down the residential street back to Rancho Viejo Road, connecting with Trabuco Creek Road to complete the final loop.

Information

Cox Sports Park

27701 Crown Valley Parkway

Ladera Ranch, CA 92694

GPS TRAILHEAD COORDINATES (WGS 84)

UTM Zone (WGS84) 11S

Easting 0437730

Northing 3710134

Latitude N 33°31'44"

Longitude W 117°40'14"

DIRECTIONS

From the merger of I-405 and I-5: Go south on I-5 for 7.8 miles and exit on Avery Parkway (Exit 85). Turn left on Avery Parkway, go under the freeway, and take the first right on Marguerite Parkway. After 0.3 miles, Marguerite Parkway becomes Rancho Viejo Road. Continue another 1 mile on Rancho Viejo Road and then turn left on Trabuco Creek Road. The ride begins on the corner of Rancho Viejo and Trabuco Creek roads, but you can't park there. Continue on Trabuco Creek Road about 100 yards to find a legal parking spot.

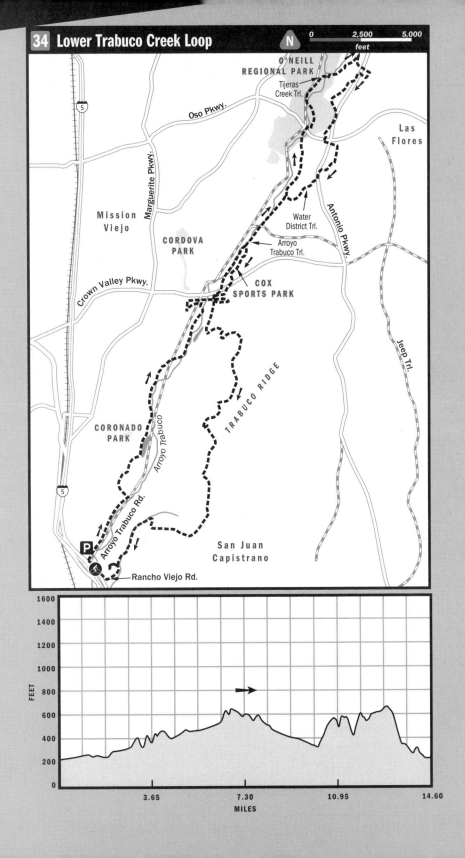

N

0   2,500   5,000
feet

O'NEILL
REGIONAL PARK

Tijeras
Creek Trl.

Las
Flores

Oso Pkwy.

5

Marguerite Pkwy.

Mission
Viejo

CORDOVA
PARK

Water
District Trl.

Antonio Pkwy.

Arroyo
Trabuco Trl.

Crown Valley Pkwy.

COX
SPORTS PARK

Jeep Trl.

TRABUCO RIDGE

CORONADO
PARK

Arroyo Trabuco

5

San Juan
Capistrano

Arroyo Trabuco Rd.

P

Rancho Viejo Rd.

Elevation profile:

1600
1400
1200
1000
800
600
400
200
0

FEET

3.65   7.30   10.95   14.60

MILES

The last whoop-de-doos on the final section of trail before Monarch Drive

Description

This ride begins and ends near Interstate 5, crossing through the final (most downstream) section of true wilderness in the Trabuco flood plain. The route exploits a few sections of fun singletrack and includes some hill climbs that are bound to make your legs burn. Although the directions above may seem complicated, once you have a general understanding of the wilderness area, the route is easy to follow. For 90 percent of the ride, you will either be in the river bottom or riding just above it. The other two major landmarks are the I-5 freeway and Crown Valley Parkway—and those are hard to miss.

For accurate mileage readings, begin at the corner of Trabuco Creek Road and Rancho Viejo Road. Ride down Trabuco Creek Road till it ends. At 0.7 miles continue past a fence toward a parking lot, but veer left on a concrete bike path before you reach the lot. The path leads to a golf course; continue straight and onto the dirt at 1.1 miles. The dirt trail edges around the driving range and then continues up Trabuco Creek. Veer left at 1.7 miles, taking the higher path. Continue straight; at 2.5 miles, the dirt road turns to a sandy singletrack as it approaches Crown Valley Parkway. Turn left at 2.8 miles, riding up the paved ramp toward the overpass. The climb ends in a residential court—turn right at 3.1 miles and then right again on Crown Valley Parkway. Ride along Crown Valley Parkway, crossing high above Trabuco Creek, then turn right on Cecil Pasture Road. Make another immediate right on a concrete pathway and wrap under Crown Valley Parkway to the Cox Sports Park.

Turn left (north) on the groomed dirt path that runs parallel to the sports park. At 4.2 miles turn left on a utility road and then immediately right on a singletrack that drops down to Arroyo Trabuco. Head right on the gravel road and keep riding: the road turns to dirt just before the Oso Parkway overpass. This marks the beginning of the Arroyo Trabuco Trail. Grind through three stream crossings, then follow the Arroyo Trabuco Trail through a canopy of live oaks.

Turn right on the Tijeras Creek Trail, just past 6 miles. Past a broad, shallow stream crossing, the singletrack winds along the creek and eventually climbs to a gate. At 6.5 miles make a hard right at the gate, riding down a groomed bike path to Antonio Parkway. Turn right on Antonio Parkway, and, at 6.8 miles, turn right on a dirt path and ride all the way to Oso Parkway. Cross Oso Parkway and head (left) through the supermarket parking lot—snacks anyone?—to Antonio Parkway. Turn right on Antonio Parkway and ride past the water district building.

Turn right on the Water District Trail, at 8 miles. The singletrack drops sharply into the canyon and then follows a BMX-like course, dipping and weaving through the trees. It's a fun trail that doesn't disappoint; you're bound to have a smile on you face when you reach the Arroyo Trabuco Trail, at 8.7 miles.

Turn left on the Arroyo Trabuco Trail and continue straight, staying in the flood plain. After crossing under Crown Valley Parkway, you'll reach a gate at 10 miles. Veer left and ride to a second gate. Turn left at the second gate and climb. Grind all the way, through a series of broad turns, to the ridgeline. Don't be fooled by turnoffs along the way—you're going to the top. You'll pass a shaded lookout on the ridge . . . keep going. The fire road drops and climbs, so use your momentum to grind up to the second lookout. The third drop leads to an even more precipitous climb, followed by a few less taxing climbs. When you reach the fourth lookout, the hard work is over. Continue a short way to a gate. Turn right at 13.2 miles and wind downhill to another gate. Turn left on Monarch Drive after 13.5 miles. Ride through the quiet neighborhood to Rancho Viejo Road and turn right. A short cruise on a bike path completes the route.

Note: This ride has less stream crossings than the Arroyo Trabuco and Tijeras Creek rides, but you will still get wet. There are restrooms and water near the geographical center of the ride at the Cox Sports Park.

MISSION VIEJO– SADDLEBACK VALLEY

35

WAGON WHEEL CANYON LOOP

KEY AT-A-GLANCE INFORMATION

Length: 3.3 miles

Configuration: Loop

Aerobic difficulty: Easy

Technical difficulty: Easy; the cumulative 1 mile of singletrack is fast but not technical.

Exposure: A few oak and sycamore groves offer shade, but most of the ride is in complete sun.

Scenery: Streambeds dotted with clusters of oaks and sycamores; vista points provide good views of the Cleveland National Forest.

Trail traffic: Light

Riding time: 30 minutes

Access: Parking at Thomas F. Riley Wilderness Park costs $3; the park is open daily, 7 a.m.–sunset. Park maps are available at the trailhead.

Special comments: Wagon Wheel Canyon is the original name for the Thomas F. Riley Wilderness Park. Street signs use both names to designate the same area. A large equestrian staging area is near the trailhead. This suggests there could be a great deal of horse traffic on the trail; however, on a Sunday afternoon in October there were no equestrians in the park.

GPS TRAILHEAD COORDINATES (WGS 84)

UTM Zone (WGS84)   11S

Easting   0444930

Northing   3714825

Latitude   N 33°34'18"

Longitude   W 117°35'36"

In Brief

This is a quick loop, using nearly all the trails in the relatively small park. Follow the Oak Canyon Trail to the Horned Toad Trail. Make the quick climb to the vista point and descend the fast singletrack back to the Oak Canyon Trail. A second short climb on the Oak Canyon Trail leads to the Mule Deer Trail. After the fun descent, head left on the Pheasant Run Trail and connect to the Wagon Wheel Canyon Trail. Veer left and climb slightly for 300 yards to trail's end, then turn around and make the quick push back to the parking lot.

Information

Thomas F. Riley Wilderness Park

30952 Oso Parkway

Coto de Caza, CA 92679

(949) 923-2265

Description

A spin through diminutive Thomas F. Riley Wilderness Park hardly ranks as an epic adventure, but the park has plenty of upside. The park is surprisingly scenic; groves of live oak and sycamores shade the park's two creek beds. The park is well maintained, and on a cloudy afternoon in October, the trails were nearly empty. This particular ride is short but contains 1 mile of fun, user-friendly

DIRECTIONS

From the intersection of the CA 405 and CA 55 freeways: Take CA 405 south 9 miles, to where the CA 405 freeway merges with the CA 5 freeway. Go south on the CA 5 freeway 5.4 miles and exit on Oso Parkway. Turn left on Oso Parkway and go 5.5 miles, passing over the CA 241 freeway. The entrance to Thomas F. Riley Wilderness Park is on the right, just before Oso Parkway ends at Coto de Caza Drive. Head through the gate and follow the dirt road 100 yards to the parking area. The trailhead is on the west end of the parking lot.

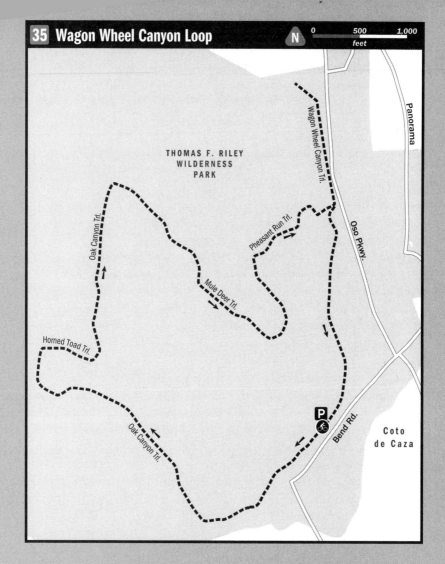

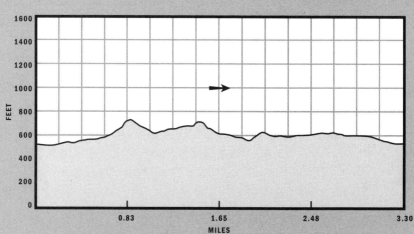

singletrack. Sure, the park is encapsulated by suburban development (vista points offer great views of the local tract homes), but did I mention the mile of empty singletrack?

The loop begins at the Oak Canyon trailhead. Head out on the Oak Canyon Trail, a dirt road, staying straight past cutoffs to the South Wagon Wheel Canyon and the Vista Ridge Trail. At 0.25 miles veer left on the scenic Sycamore Loop. Before you know it, you are back on the Oak Canyon Trail. A short grade leads to the Horned Toad Trail. Just before 0.7 miles veer left on the Horned Toad Trail and follow the doubletrack to the vista point. This is the steepest climb of the ride, but it's only a short distance to the route's highest point. The peaks of Saddleback loom above the vista point, and the Coto de Caza housing development lies below. Ironically, Coto de Caza means game preserve in Portuguese. Even though mountain-lion warning signs are ubiquitous throughout this wilderness park, most of the local game is probably of the canine variety these days.

Head down the Horned Toad Trail. The trail, now a singletrack, is somewhat steep but easily managed. At the bottom, turn left on the Oak Canyon Trail and follow the road as it meanders uphill. At 1.5 miles the Oak Canyon Trail becomes the Vista Ridge Trail. If you feel like climbing a bit more, continue up the Vista Ridge Trail to Skink Vista Point, but otherwise turn right on the Mule Deer Trail. The trail runs fast, and you'll be tempted to push hard through the wide-open turns. Just past a flat wooden bridge, the old trail appears to be washed out and closed. A replacement trail completes the downhill. At 1.9 miles turn left (away from a parking lot) on the unsigned Pheasant Run Trail. Follow the trail as it weaves its way through a meadow. At 2.2 miles the trail splits, but both branches run headlong into the tree-lined creek bed. Either way, a short hike is required to cross the creek (which is generally dry). At 2.3 miles head left on Wagon Wheel Canyon Trail. Follow the trail as it courses parallel to Oso Parkway. Near 2.6 miles the trail ends at the wilderness-park boundary. At this point, turn around and return along the trail—cranking along through the trees, across a small culvert, and soon reaching the parking lot. And that's it. After a whopping 3.3 miles and 400 feet of climbing you may want to do the loop again. For variety you may want to ride the Vista Ridge Trail to the Mule Deer Trail.

After the Ride

There are several casual eateries in the Mission Market Place on Oso Parkway. None of them come highly recommended. A nicer option might be to bring a lunch and eat in scenic Wagon Wheel Canyon. There is a nice picnic area under the trees next to the parking area. After lunch you may be tempted to take a stroll through the butterfly garden. The best months for viewing the butterflies are in late spring and early summer. In other months you might find hummingbirds hovering near the native plants.

36

| COTO TO CASPERS RIDE

KEY AT-A-GLANCE INFORMATION

Length: 21.5 miles

Configuration: 15 miles out-and-back (7.5 miles each way) with 6.5-mile loop

Aerobic difficulty: Moderate to difficult; a relatively long ride with plenty of short, steep climbs

Technical difficulty: Easy; all open fire road. This is a good training ride; however, there is a dearth of challenging downhill action.

Exposure: Complete sun with mere snippets of shade

Scenery: Views of suburbia near the trailhead, then rolling hills and classic canyon landscapes with live oaks and chaparral

Trail traffic: Moderate (or more) near the trailhead and light in Caspers Wilderness Park

Riding time: 2–3 hours

Access: Parallel park on Dove Canyon Drive near Santa Margarita High School. The ride follows a hiking/equestrian trail from Coto de Caza into Caspers Wilderness Park.

In Brief

Skirt through Coto de Caza on the Bell View Trail. Connect to the West Ridge Trail, rolling through the northern end of Caspers Wilderness Park. Drop down the Starr Rise Trail to Bell Canyon. Loop clockwise, following Bell Canyon. Climb the Oso Trail toward Cougar Pass, then make a sharp climb up the Sun Rise Trail to the East Ridge. A rolling drop leads to the head of Bell Canyon. Crank up pavement and then dirt back to Starr Rise Trail. Make the steep climb back to the West Ridge Trail and retrace the rolling terrain back to the trailhead.

Information

Caspers Wilderness Park
33401 Ortega Highway
San Juan Capistrano, CA 92675
(949) 923-2210

Description

The rolling hills of Caspers Wilderness Park surround the Ortega Highway corridor near the southern border of Orange County. The park gained notoriety in 1986, when a 5-year-old girl, hiking with her mother, was mauled by a mountain lion. The mother claimed she should have been warned about mountain-lion risks and her resulting lawsuit raised a storm of public debate. Eventually, the mother won a two million dollar judgment. Consequently,

GPS TRAILHEAD COORDINATES (WGS 84)

UTM Zone (WGS84) 11S
Easting 0446418
Northing 3722668
Latitude N 33°38'33"
Longitude W 117°34'40"

DIRECTIONS

From the intersection of the CA 405 and CA 133 freeways: Take CA 405 south toward San Diego. After 2 miles I-405 merges with CA 5 freeway. Follow CA 5 south 3.2 miles and exit at Alicia Parkway. Turn left on Alicia Parkway, go 5.3 miles, and turn right on Santa Margarita Parkway. After 2.6 miles, turn right on Plano Trabuco Road. The first left is Dove Canyon Drive. Park in the first available spot; the trailhead is near the corner of Dove Canyon Drive and Plano Trabuco Road, next to a waterfall.

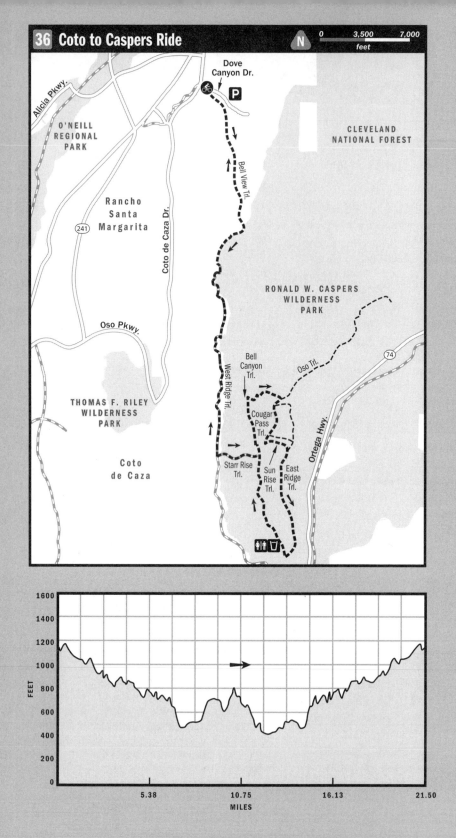

there are now warning signs for mountain lions in all local parks, even parks where nary a cougar has been sited.

Mountain lions do still roam the hills of Caspers Wilderness Park (a bulletin board lists the latest sightings) and several other adjacent wilderness areas. Their presence is worth noting: two mountain bikers were attacked (one fatally) in nearby Whiting Ranch in 2004. Cyclists should be vigilant, riding in groups whenever possible, but not paranoid. Two attacks in over 20 years does not constitute a trend. There is a risk of mountain-lion attacks, but it is miniscule compared to the risks one takes while driving on the freeway.

This ride accesses the park from Coto de Caza, the suburban community that spawned the quasi-reality television show *The Real Housewives of Orange County*. Start up the paved ramp near the waterfall. After a quick climb turn right on a dirt pathway. The groomed trail passes a series of homes—some castlelike, others merely ostentatious. Watch out for pedestrians: this is a popular spot for Coto de Caza residents to walk their dogs. After 1 mile, pass through a gap in a fence on your right and follow a parallel trail. This trail will have less traffic.

Soon you will be in Caspers Wilderness Park. Follow the West Ridge Trail, heading generally downhill on the rolling dirt road. At 2.5 miles there is a rest area with shade and water. You may need this on the way back. You'll reach gates at 3.7 miles and at 5 miles. The route is obvious—stay on the West Ridge Trail.

At 6.5 miles turn left on the Starr Rise Trail. If you're not sure, a sign explains that this is the only mountain bike access to Bell Canyon. Cruise down the Starr Rise Trail; a couple of spurs may lead you off route. Just follow the bike tracks. The Starr Rise Trail ends at a T-junction with the Bell Canyon Trail. This is where the loop part of the route begins. Turn left at 7.5 miles and ride up the canyon. Several mature trees provide a nice respite from the sun. Enjoy, because this is the only significant shade to be found on the ride. Watch out for equestrians—the horses like the shade as well.

Turn right on the Oso Trail, at 8.2 miles, and begin to climb. It's a short, steep haul to the Cougar Pass Trail. At 8.9 miles turn right on the Cougar Pass Trail and head briefly downhill. Turn left on the Sun Rise Trail at 9.7 miles. A beastly climb leads to the East Ridge Trail. When you make the ridge, turn right and glide down the length of the rolling descent.

The East Ridge Trail ends at the Bell Canyon Trail, here a paved road. Turn right at 12 miles. Water, restrooms, and a park map are just ahead on the left. Follow the pavement, past a couple of campgrounds. At 12.7 miles head through a gate and get back onto dirt. Crank up the canyon to complete the loop. Turn left on the Starr Rise Trail, at 14 miles, and make the steep climb back to the ridge.

Turn right on the West Ridge Trail, at 15 miles, and retrace the route back to the trailhead. The way back is generally uphill, so pace yourself and don't bonk. At 17.8 miles you'll have the option to follow a singletrack that runs parallel to the West Ridge Trail. This option doesn't reduce the amount of climbing, but it allows for a slightly fun diversion. The rest area with shade and water comes at 19 miles. You'll thank the Boy Scout who built it.

You'll reach the Dove Canyon waterfalls at 21.5 miles. Jumping in is not recommended.

Note: All trails in Caspers Wilderness Park will be closed after significant rainfall. Conversely, the region bakes in the summer months (which generally includes spring and fall in Southern California). Bring plenty of water.

ORTEGA HIGHWAY-
SAN JUAN TRAIL

UPPER SAN JUAN LOOP

KEY AT-A-GLANCE INFORMATION

Length: 8.4 miles

Configuration: Loop

Aerobic difficulty: Moderate

Technical difficulty: Moderate to difficult; most of the rocky sections are climbs. The Old San Juan Trail has some bike-swallowing ruts.

Exposure: More shade than sun

Scenery: Rolling, unfettered wilderness and more manzanita than you can shake a stick at

Trail traffic: Moderate; the San Juan Trail is a popular weekend jaunt for many local riders.

Riding time: 1.25–2 hours

Access: The entire ride takes place in the Cleveland National Forest. There are a few parking spots in the dirt near the trailhead. If those are full, park on one of the spurs along Lost Canyon Road or near Blue Jay Campground. There is no payment kiosk, so you will need an Adventure Pass to park. Daily or annual Adventure Passes may be purchased on the U.S. Forest Service Web site or at local sporting-goods stores such as Sportmart, Big 5, and Sport Chalet. Check the Forest Service Web site for a dealer near you.

GPS TRAILHEAD COORDINATES (WGS 84)

UTM Zone (WGS84) 11S

Easting 0458421

Northing 3723698

Latitude N 33°38'08"

Longitude W 117°26'54"

In Brief

Get out of your car and start riding singletrack. Follow the varied, and sometimes challenging, terrain of the San Juan Trail all the way to Cocktail Rock. Instead of continuing down the San Juan Trail, turn right on the Old San Juan Trail. The old trail climbs slightly and then makes a harrowing drop before climbing back to the main trail. Backtrack a short distance on the San Juan Trail and then follow the Old San Juan Trail to North Main Divide Road. A short ride through Blue Jay Campground leads back to the trailhead. (Note: if you need a warm-up or some time to dial in your bike, take a loop around Blue Jay Campground.)

Information

Cleveland National Forest—Trabuco Ranger District
Keith Fletcher, District Ranger
1147 East Sixth Street
Corona, CA 92879
(951) 736-1811

Blue Jay Campground
(909) 736-1811

Description

The Upper San Juan Loop provides a great alternative for riders who don't want to ride the entire San Juan Trail out and back (22 miles of singletrack), or make the somewhat logistically complicated and time-consuming one-way ride on the trail with a car shuttle back to the trailhead.

DIRECTIONS

From the intersection of the CA 405 and CA 5 freeways: Head south on CA 5 11.2 miles and take the Ortega Highway exit. Turn left at the stoplight and follow Ortega Highway 23.2 miles to Long Canyon Road. Turn left on Long Canyon Road and continue uphill 4.5 miles to the trailhead.

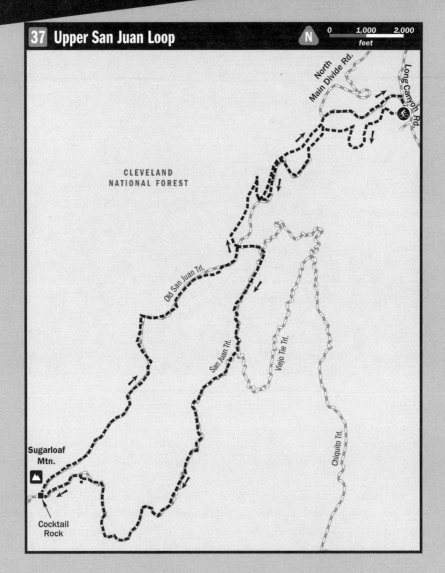

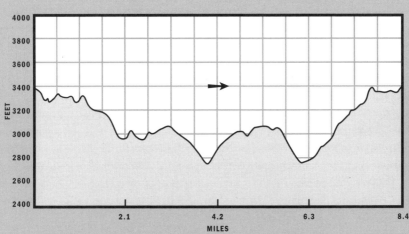

Marko emerges from the manzanita

The loop is merely 8.4 miles, but it's 8.4 miles of great singletrack, which follows varied terrain and is chock full of rip-roaring downhills, rock gardens, switchbacks, bushwhacking, and amazing scenery. Of course, there is a bit of climbing as well, but the reward is well worth the effort.

The initial section of the San Juan Trail traverses a rock-strewn hillside. The trail is rocky and bumpy from the get-go, but, aside from one small washout, it's all makeable. Stay straight at 1.4 miles, passing the Old San Juan Trail. The trail begins to drop down. Rip through the trees and head straight at another junction at 1.9 miles. After 2 miles continue straight past the Chiquito Trail. You'll pass the turnoff for the Viejo Tie Trail at 2.6 miles. Stay on the San Juan Trail, climb a bit, then drop down a smooth and fast section of trail.

After 4 miles you'll begin the climb to Cocktail Rock. It's a challenging ascent with a few tight switchbacks and plenty of rocks. Expect to walk a bit unless you have flawless skills. Try to stay on the bike as much as possible. Full-suspension riders may benefit by stiffening their suspensions (particularly for larger riders, to avoid bottoming out on the rocks; light riders, women, and children need not worry).

You'll reach Cocktail Rock (sometimes called Lunch Rock) at 4.9 miles. This is the final intersection of the San Juan and the Old San Juan trails. It is also a popular stopping point for just about every person who rides the trail. From this point the San Juan Trail runs southwest, dropping nearly continuously to San Juan Hot Springs.

Turn right and follow the Old San Juan Trail northeast. The trail climbs intermittently over mounds of decomposed granite. You'll begin a rapid descent at 5.6 miles. There is a reason they call it the Old San Juan Trail . . . it's not really maintained. Keep a high line, because there are ruts large enough to hold a family of four. The bushes may get somewhat intrusive in places as well. Don't pay too much heed to these concerns, though. Just go. It's a fun, challenging, and—at high speed—harrowing descent.

Past 6.1 miles the trail bottoms out near Chiquito Spring. Continue cranking along the trail, climbing moderately, till you reach an intersection, at 6.8 miles, with the San Juan Trail. Here turn left. You'll remember this section from before, but going uphill you'll have a chance to take in the scenery that blurred by before. Turn left at 7.2 miles, once again catching the Old San Juan Trail. The trail clears the trees and climbs a hillside of scrub brush and manzanita. Near 8 miles you'll reach the junction with North Main Divide Road. From this point you may either stay straight and wind your way through Blue Jay Campground back to the trailhead or turn right and follow a short connector trail and then retrace the first section of the San Juan Trail back to the trailhead.

Note: Much of the soil on the San Juan Trail is decomposed granite, so this is good ride for days when other trails are too muddy. There is some poison oak on the trail. Be mindful of rubbing your face in the bushes. You might also consider bringing some isopropyl alcohol along just to be safe (it's a long drive home to your shower).

After the Ride

Find your way to Las Golondrinas. The deli-style Mexican restaurant is in the business center near the CA 5 freeway (on the south side of Ortega Highway). Look forward to some of the best Mexican food in Orange County—fresh tamales, fish burritos, carnitas, and nopalitos. Don't miss it.

Las Golondrinas
27124 Paseo Espada #803
San Juan Capistrano, CA 92675
(949) 240-3440

38

SAN JUAN TRAIL (LOWER SECTION)

KEY AT-A-GLANCE INFORMATION

Length: 12.5 miles

Configuration: Out-and-back

Aerobic difficulty: Somewhat strenuous

Technical difficulty: Moderate to difficult; nothing steep, but the narrow singletrack has plenty of rocks, ruts, and tight switchbacks.

Exposure: Mostly full sun

Scenery: Steep granite hillsides covered in chaparral and manzanita

Trail traffic: Light on weekdays, moderate on weekends. Be mindful of other trail users; the path is narrow with lots of blind turns.

Riding time: 1.75–2.75 hours

Access: The entire ride takes place in the Cleveland National Forest. Parking in the dirt lot near the trailhead costs $5. There is a payment kiosk adjacent to the restrooms in case you don't have an Adventure Pass. Daily or annual Adventure Passes may be purchased on the U.S. Forest Service Web site or at local sporting-goods stores such as Sportmart, Big 5, and Sport Chalet. Check the Forest Service Web site for a dealer near you.

In Brief

The directions are simple: follow the San Juan Trail to Cocktail Rock and return. The outbound ride runs almost completely uphill. You won't reach a trail fork until you reach Cocktail Rock. The return trip is a hoot, an adrenaline rush, a great test of your biking skills, and definitely worth the climb.

Description

The San Juan Trail is Orange County's most famous singletrack. For more than 20 years, the trail has been a key destination (perhaps a pilgrimage) for every serious mountain biker in the area. The trail's popularity, as well as a slew of El Niño winters, have caused it to wear down a bit, but it's still not to be missed. Although the route has become more rocky and technical over the years, it remains well suited for mountain biking and hiking.

Many San Juan riders shuttle the trail, starting at Blue Jay Campground and riding down. It's the fastest way to ride the entire trail, but you waste a lot of time in the car that could be better spent on the trail (particularly considering the current construction project on Ortega Highway, slated to go on till fall of 2008). The ride up to Cocktail Rock is technical but not grueling. The challenges of the terrain and the scenery will make you forget the effort of the climb. So why not start from the bottom and earn it?

GPS TRAILHEAD COORDINATES (WGS 84)

UTM Zone (WGS84)   11S
Easting   0452670
Northing   3718095
Latitude   N 33°36'06"
Longitude   W 117°30'37"

DIRECTIONS

From the intersection of the CA 405 and CA 5 freeways: Head south on CA 5 11.2 miles and take the Ortega Highway exit. Turn left at the light and follow Ortega Highway 12.5 miles. A hand-painted sign for Lazy W Ranch (just before the San Juan fire station) marks the beginning of Hot Springs Canyon Road. Turn left and follow the dirt road 0.9 miles to a shady parking lot.

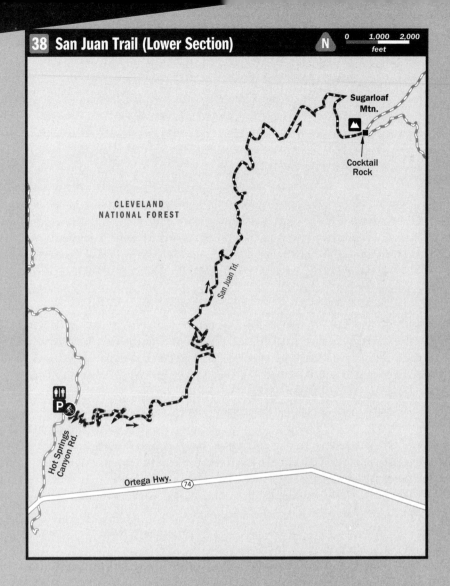

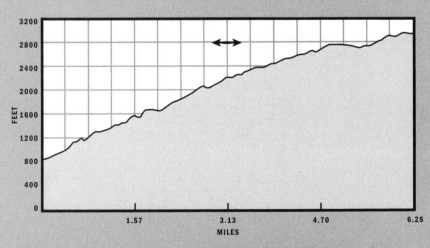

The trail climbs immediately. You may want to warm up on Hot Springs Canyon Road before jumping on the singletrack. If you warm up on the canyon road, you're bound to encounter a few dogs, barking madly. Fortunately, at this writing, they are well restrained.

From the trailhead, the singletrack switchbacks steeply out of the canyon. Most of the switchbacks are near the trailhead, perhaps 20 in the first mile. Keep your momentum, shift your weight forward, and see how many of the tight turns you can clean. In a short time you will be well above the canyon.

As the switchbacks grow less frequent, the trail becomes a bit more rocky and rutted. Use your suspension and power through the obstacles. Near 2 miles the route crosses a saddle, running high above Ortega Highway. You'll encounter some steep sections with a surface of loose, decomposed granite that seems to defy traction. There are also a couple of washed-out turns. Don't worry, though—any walking or portaging will be short-lived.

Keep coursing along the trail. It's all gradually uphill, except for one short downhill at 4.7 miles, until you reach Cocktail Rock at 6.3 miles. If you want to continue on the San Juan Trail, head right—it's another 5 miles to Blue Jay Campground (this extension will add 10 miles to the route). Your other option is to head left and down the Old San Juan Trail. Following the Old San Juan Trail to its intersection with the San Juan Trail and looping back to Cocktail Rock will add 5 miles to the ride. Read the description of Ride 37, Upper San Juan Loop (page 164) for trail directions and conditions for the Old San Juan Trail and the upper section of the San Juan Trail.

Of course there is nothing wrong with riding to Cocktail Rock and then retracing to the trailhead—in fact, it's a great ride. The ride down is a rush, with plenty of obstacles and course problems to keep you on the edge of your bike seat. There are also plenty of blind turns, so be mindful of other trail users and stay in control. Also, stay on the trail: don't add yourself to the list of riders who have ridden off the side of the San Juan Trail.

The final challenge is to make all the switchbacks. Turns you couldn't make on the way up will be easier at speed. Keep your momentum. If you miss a few, don't be discouraged—there are plenty more to hone your skills on. By the time you reach the bottom, you'll be a veteran switchback rider.

Note: The decomposed granite on the San Juan Trail rides well in wet conditions. There isn't much poison oak on the lower half of the trail, but if you venture beyond Cocktail Rock you might encounter a bit of the leafy menace. If you are sensitive poison oak, consider bringing alcohol wipes or a bottle of alcohol (isopropyl, not tequila) along in the car.

DANA POINT AND SAN CLEMENTE

39

DANA HILLS LOOP

Length: 5.5 miles

Configuration: Double loop

Aerobic difficulty: Easy to moderate; a couple of short, steep climbs

Technical difficulty: Variable; predominantly smooth and easy fire road, punctuated with a couple of steep singletrack sections

Exposure: Complete sun

Scenery: Red-tile rooftops and ridgelines still, thankfully, spared from grading

Trail traffic: Light

Riding time: 1 hour or less

Access: Free street parking is available near the trailhead. Look on Via Madrina, which is off La Novia Avenue one block north of Via Entrada; or park on San Juan Creek Road (there is a wide dirt shoulder where the street abuts the San Juan Hills Golf Course).

Special comments: You may have to share some of the fire roads with motorcycles, so be careful. Fortunately, the singletrack riding seems to be left for cyclists.

In Brief

Climb up Via Entrada and then veer left on an unnamed fire road into Dana Hills. Crank up to the ridge and bear right, following a semicircular path above the gated community of San Juan Hills. When you reach the west side of the rooftops (and before the road heads down), turn left on another unnamed fire road. There are plenty of riding options here, including some fun singletrack. Another left turn puts you on a ridge above a reservoir. Follow a singletrack, and then a dirt road, counterclockwise along the ridge above the reservoir. Drop down to another singletrack and traverse the hillside above the reservoir. A final steep drop leads back to the first fire road you rode after Via Entrada. Continue west and downhill. A final singletrack drops down to La Novia Avenue. A short ride on the street completes the loop.

Description

Dana Hills or Dana Point Hills is a compact swath of open space wedged between San Clemente, Dana Point, and the sprawling outreach of San Juan Capistrano. Drive out to the San Juan Trail (see Rides 37 and 38), and you'll see this small clump of ridges just as you exit the CA 5 freeway. It is by no means impressive backcountry and probably will never be a "destination" mountain biking spot. However, for area riders, Dana Hills offers a nice diversion and the opportunity for some quality after-work training rides.

GPS TRAILHEAD COORDINATES (WGS 84)

UTM Zone (WGS84)   11S
Easting   0440108
Northing   3706467
Latitude   N 33°29'46"
Longitude   W 117°38'41"

DIRECTIONS

From the intersection of the CA 405 and CA 5 freeways: Go south on CA 5 11.1 miles. Exit at Ortega Highway (CA 74) and turn left. After 0.5 miles turn right on La Novia Avenue. Continue 0.6 miles on La Novia Avenue to Via Entrada (you will cross San Juan Creek Road and pass Via Madrina). See Access, above, for parking recommendations.

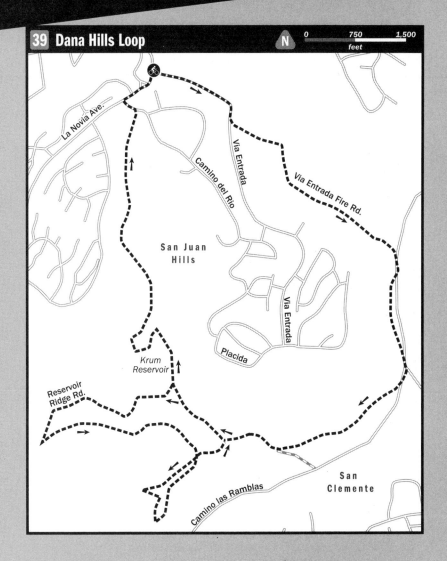

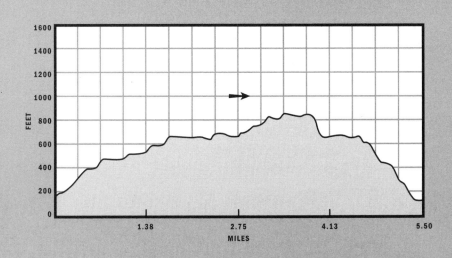

Don't worry if you are confused by the brief directions above; Dana Hills is small and relatively easy to navigate. A couple of ridgeline fire roads course through the riding area. Luckily there are several fun and somewhat challenging singletracks that connect to the fire roads. As you rip down the trails, two obvious landmarks—the Krum Reservoir and the San Juan Hills housing development—will keep you on course. You should view this loop as a template for possible mountain biking routes in the area. As you ride and explore Dana Hills, allow yourself the opportunity to try different trails and different routes.

Begin on the east side of Via Entrada and climb on the sidewalk. Turn left on a fire road after 0.2 miles. Continue straight as the road runs paved for a short span. At 0.5 miles head right on a dirt road. Crank up a steep hill, ascending above the red-tile roofs of San Juan Hills. Stay right on the ridge at 1.2 miles. Crank hard on the short downhills and use your momentum to carry you over the climbs. Veer right at 1.8 miles. You'll see some steep singletrack straight ahead: that comes later.

At 2.1 miles turn left, and away from the houses, on a new fire road. Follow this road to the 2.5-mile point and then make a hard left, climbing a short span of singletrack to the ridgetop. You'll see the Krum Reservoir below you on the right. Keep following the ridge, counterclockwise, around the reservoir basin. Veer right and stay on the ridge at 3 miles. You'll make two more short climbs. Then, at 3.3 miles, turn right and drop down a single-track. After 50 yards the trail intersects with another singletrack at a T junction. Turn right and traverse the curving hillside (now riding clockwise above the reservoir) until the trail runs back up to the ridgetop. Continue straight on the singletrack at 3.6 miles and plunge down (on the singletrack you saw earlier) to the fire road above San Juan Hills.

Turn left at 3.7 miles and stay straight on the dirt road at 4.1 miles. You'll pick up speed as the road winds downhill. Don't miss the final trail, though: turn right at 4.8 miles and careen down the fast singletrack to La Novia Avenue. Turn right on La Novia Avenue and spin down the road to complete the loop.

After the Ride

Head to downtown San Juan Capistrano and try El Campion. You'll find the meat market/tortilleria/taqueria in the El Adobe Center, just blocks from the train station and the mission. The food is authentic and unadulterated, probably not recommended for the diet conscious and the health minded, but it's good. Expect a long line at the counter during lunchtime.

El Campion
31921 Camino Capistrano #15
San Juan Capistrano, CA
(949) 489-9767

40

SAN MATEO CANYON LOOP

KEY AT-A-GLANCE INFORMATION

Length: 7.7 miles

Configuration: Loop

Aerobic difficulty: Moderate; one steep climb; several short pushes

Technical difficulty: Moderate; the singletrack will challenge your bike-handling skills, but none of the sections are scary.

Exposure: Complete sun with mere smidgens of shade

Scenery: Christianitos Creek and the hills of Camp Pendleton

Trail traffic: Light; watch for hikers and dog walkers on the Rancho San Clemente Ridgeline Trail.

Riding time: 50 minutes–1.5 hours

Access: Free street parking is available on Avenida La Pata (next to the dog park). San Mateo Creek is part of San Onofre State Park.

Special comments: The hills on the far side of San Mateo Creek are part of Camp Pendleton and therefore closed to public access.

In Brief

Head south past the dog park, following a groomed path to the first set of utility towers. Turn left and head downhill. The trail—which begins as a doubletrack and then narrows to a singletrack—drops toward San Mateo Creek. Keep heading south and rip through every section of trail until you reach Christianitos Road. Turn left on the road and then reconnect to and retrace a section of the singletrack. After 3.7 miles turn left on an unnamed fire road and climb to the ridge. At road's end, jump on the State Park Connector Trail and climb the rugged singletrack all the way to Rancho San Clemente Ridgeline Trail. Climb the paved trail up to a water tank. The way back is all downhill and paved. Follow Rancho San Clemente Ridgeline Trail to a second tank and then turn right and drop to a skate park. A short ride down Avenida La Pata finishes the loop.

Description

The highlight of this ride is a network of fun singletrack that runs through San Onofre State Park—the domain of surfing, nude sunbathing, and nuclear power. Not far from its legendary beaches, San Onofre State Park manages a corridor of riparian wilderness along San Mateo Creek. The land is actually leased from Camp Pendleton in an effort to preserve a vital section of local wetlands. Unfortunately, the myopic Transportation Corridor Agency plans to extend the Foothill South toll road down the length of the San Mateo watershed. The construction, which is facing several legal challenges, would impact some of the trails in this ride.

GPS TRAILHEAD COORDINATES (WGS 84)

UTM Zone (WGS84) 11S
Easting 0445967
Northing 3700890
Latitude N 33°26'46"
Longitude W 117°34'53"

DIRECTIONS

From the intersection of the CA 5 freeway and the Pacific Coast Highway: Go south on I-5 3 miles and exit at Avenida Pico. Turn left on Avenida Pico, go 1.8 miles, and turn right on Avenida La Pata. Follow Avenida La Pata 1.4 miles to its end. The trailhead is just left of the adjacent dog park.

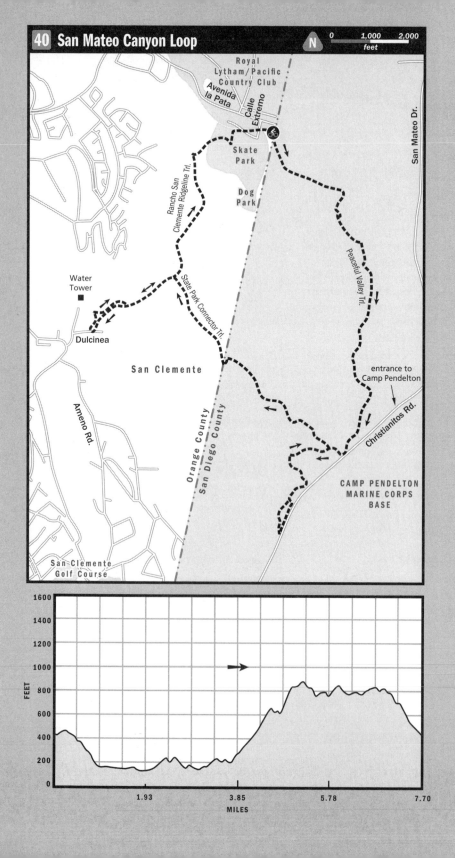

The mountain biking in the state park runs through a section of San Mateo Canyon between Talega Golf Course and Christianitos Road. There are several tame multiuse trails here, as well as a tight web of twisting mountain bike trails. The latter trails are quite fun—seemingly made by mountain bikers with delusions of BMX grandeur. Don't worry, the trails are legal: they are listed on the posted maps but, in most cases, not named.

There is plenty of singletrack to explore in San Mateo Canyon. This ride is just one of many route options. Don't hesitate to explore. As long as you know the general geography of the area, it is difficult to get lost. Posted maps at the trailhead show all the major trails as well as roads and the placement of utility towers. Oddly, the trails have all been given long and difficult-to-pronounce Polynesian names. Ignore these names (unless you're Polynesian) and simply use geographical markers for guidance.

Turn right past the dog park and follow the groomed trail to a group of four utility towers. Head left, at 0.25 miles, and charge downhill. Past the last tower, the trail narrows to singletrack and winds through a lush hillside arroyo. After 0.5 miles turn right on a second singletrack. This is the Peaceful Valley Trail, but the riding experience is far from tranquil. Rip through a series of arroyos and over small hills. The trail will keep you on edge as it careens, dips, and weaves along the tight course.

Stay on the singletrack, continuing straight across a dirt road at 2.2 miles. Continue straight again, at 2.8 miles—eventually the trail will run out at Christianitos Road. Turn left on the road, past 2.9 miles, and then left again on a dirt road at 3.1 miles. Climb a few yards on the road, then turn right on singletrack. You've already ridden this section of trail, but it's fun in both directions.

Turn left on a dirt fire road, at 3.7 miles, and crank uphill. At 4.3 miles stay left (a right turn will take you back to the trailhead) and keep climbing. Turn right, at 4.5 miles, on the State Park Connector Trail. This rugged trail drops and then climbs steeply to the ridge. (Keep this connector trail in mind for another ride—it's a fun downhill!). At 5 miles turn right on the paved Rancho San Clemente Ridgeline (RSCR) Trail and ride to a picnic bench. Head left and uphill from the bench, and follow a dirt trail back to the RSCR Trail. Turn right, at 5.3 miles, and climb to where the trail ends at a water tower.

The rest of the ride is paved and generally downhill. Retrace the RSCR Trail back to the picnic bench, and then continue straight to a second water tank. Just downhill from the second tank, at 7.2 miles, turn right on a narrow, paved trail. This trail drops sharply to a skate park. If you're up to it, challenge the skaters on the ramps. Otherwise, head through the parking lot back to Avenida La Pata. Finish the loop at the dog park, which is just downhill.

After the Ride

If the weather is nice, head down to San Clemente pier and try the Fisherman's Restaurant and Bar. The restaurant serves breakfast, lunch, and dinner on its patio just above the surf line. The food is pretty good, and the view is even better.

Fisherman's Restaurant and Bar

611 Avenida Victoria

San Clemente, CA 92672

(949) 498-6390

APPENDIXES AND INDEX

APPENDIX A:
ORANGE COUNTY
BIKE SHOPS BY LOCATON

Anaheim

Big Wheel Bicycles
919 South Euclid Street
Anaheim 92802
(714) 956-5564

Rock and Road Cyclery
5701 Santa Ana Canyon Road, Suite F&G
Anaheim Hills 92807
(714) 998-2453
www.rocknroadcyclery.net

Brea

Two Wheeler Dealer Bicycles
1039 East Imperial Highway #f-3
Brea 92821
(714) 671-1730
www.twdcycling.com

Buena Park

Buena Park Bicycle Co.
6042 Beach Boulevard
Buena Park 90621
(714) 521-8120
www.fullertonbicycle.com

Costa Mesa

Cycle Werks
2937 South Bristol Street, Suite D100
Costa Mesa 92626
(714) 751-9551
www.cyclewerks.net

Two Wheels One Planet
420 East 17th Street
Costa Mesa 92627
(949) 646-7706
www.twowheelsoneplanet.com

Cypress

Bikeland
5530 Lincoln Avenue
Cypress 90630
(714) 995-6541

Dana Point

Revo Cycles
34155 Pacific Coast Highway
Dana Point 92629
(949) 496-1995
www.revocycles.com

Fountain Valley

Bicycle Discovery
8800 Warner Avenue
Fountain Valley 92708
(714) 841-1366

Performance Bike
8850 Warner Avenue
Fountain Valley 92708
(714) 842-3480

Fullerton

Banning's Bikes
206 North Harbor Boulevard
Fullerton 92832
(714) 525-2200

The Bicycle Lane
225 East Orangethorpe Avenue
Fullerton 92832
(714) 773-0004

Fullerton Bicycle Co.
424 East Commonwealth Avenue
Fullerton 92832
(714) 879-8310
www.fullertonbicycle.com

Jax Bicycle Center
2520 East Chapman Avenue
Fullerton 92831
(714) 441-1100
www.jaxbicycles.com

Garden Grove

Richard's Cyclery
11943 Valley View Street
Garden Grove 92845
(714) 379-2717

Huntington Beach

Huntington Beach Bicycles
15862 Springdale Street
Huntington Beach 92647
(714) 892-5519
www.hbbikes.com

Jax Bicycle Center
401 Main Street
Huntington Beach 92648
(714) 969-8684
www.jaxbicycles.com

REI
7777 Edinger Avenue
Huntington Beach 92647
(714) 379-1938
www.rei.com

Surf City Cyclery
7470 Edinger Avenue
Huntington Beach 92647
(714) 842-1717
www.surfcitycyclery.com

Irvine

Rock and Road Cyclery
6282 Irvine Boulevard
Irvine 92620
(949) 733-2453
www.rocknroadcyclery.net

Sand Canyon Cyclery
6616 Irvine Center Drive
Irvine 92618
(949) 450-9906
www.sandcanyoncyclery.com

Ladera Ranch

Ladera Cyclery
25662 Crown Valley Parkway H-2
Ladera Ranch 92694
(949) 429-7784
www.laderacyclery.com

Laguna Beach

Laguna Cyclery
240 Thalia Street
Laguna Beach 92651
(949) 494-1522
www.lagunacyclery.net

Rainbow Bicycle Company
485 North Coast Highway
Laguna Beach 92651
(949) 497-5806
www.teamrain.com

Laguna Hills

Performance Bike
24721 Alicia Parkway
Laguna Hills 92653
(949) 707-0344

Laguna Niguel

Rock and Road Cyclery
27281 La Paz Road, Suite N
Laguna Niguel 92677
(949) 360-8045
www.rocknroadcyclery.net

Laguna Woods

Edge Cycle Sports
2352 Moulton Parkway #107
Laguna Woods 92657
(800) 698-3343
www.edgecyclesports.com

Lake Forest

Two Wheels One Planet
24844 Muirlands Boulevard
Lake Forest 92638
(949) 581-8900
www.twowheelsoneplanet.com

Mission Viejo

Cycle Werks
27672 Crown Valley Parkway
Mission Viejo 92691
(949) 364-5771
www.cyclewerks.net

Rock and Road Cyclery
27825 Santa Margarita Parkway, Suite A
Mission Viejo 92691
(949) 859-5076
www.rocknroadcyclery.net

Orange

Orange Cycle
210 South Glassel
Orange 92866
(714) 532-6838
www.orangecycle.com

Switchback Cyclery
3436 East Chapman Avenue
Orange 92869
(714) 628-3913
www.switchbackcyclery.com

San Clemente

Cycle Werks
1421 North El Camino Real
San Clemente 92672
(949) 492-5911
www.cyclewerks.net

San Clemente Cyclery
2801 South El Camino Real
San Clemente 92672
(949) 492-8890
www.sccyclery.com

Santa Ana

REI
1411 South Village Way
Santa Ana 92705
(714) 543-4142
www.rei.com

Tustin

The Path Bike Shop
215 West First Street
Tustin 92780
(714) 669-0784
www.thepathbikeshop.com

Performance Bike
2745 El Camino Real
Tustin 92782
(714) 838-0641

Santiago Cycling
115 North Prospect
Tustin 92780
(714) 544-6091
www.cyclingpros.com

Yorba Linda

Jax Bicycle Center
17593 Yorba Linda Boulevard
Yorba Linda 92886
(714) 996-9093

APPENDIX B: ORANGE COUNTY BIKE SHOPS BY NAME

Banning's Bikes
206 North Harbor Boulevard
Fullerton 92832
(714) 525-2200

Bicycle Discovery
8800 Warner Avenue
Fountain Valley 92708
(714) 841-1366

The Bicycle Lane
225 East Orangethorpe Avenue
Fullerton 92832
(714) 773-0004

Big Wheel Bicycles
919 South Euclid Street
Anaheim 92802
(714) 956-5564

Bikeland
5530 Lincoln Avenue
Cypress 90630
(714) 995-6541

Buena Park Bicycle Co.
6042 Beach Boulevard
Buena Park 90621
(714) 521-8120
www.fullertonbicycle.com

Cycle Werks
27672 Crown Valley Parkway
Mission Viejo 92691
(949) 364-5771
www.cyclewerks.net

Cycle Werks
1421 North El Camino Real
San Clemente 92672
(949) 492-5911
www.cyclewerks.net

Cycle Werks
2937 South Bristol Street, Suite D100
Costa Mesa 92626
(714) 751-9551
www.cyclewerks.net

Edge Cycle Sports
2352 Moulton Parkway #107
Laguna Woods 92657
(800) 698-3343
www.edgecyclesports.com

Fullerton Bicycle Co.
424 East Commonwealth Avenue
Fullerton 92832
(714) 879-8310
www.fullertonbicycle.com

Huntington Beach Bicycles
15862 Springdale Street
Huntington Beach 92647
(714) 892-5519
www.hbbikes.com

Jax Bicycle Center
2520 East Chapman Avenue
Fullerton 92831
(714) 441-1100
www.jaxbicycles.com

Jax Bicycle Center
401 Main Street
Huntington Beach 92648
(714) 969-8684
www.jaxbicycles.com

Jax Bicycle Center
14280 Culver Drive
Irvine 92604
(949) 733-1212
www.jaxbicycles.com

Jax Bicycle Center
17593 Yorba Linda Boulevard
Yorba Linda 92886
(714) 996-9093

Ladera Cyclery
25662 Crown Valley Parkway H-2
Ladera Ranch 92694
(949) 429-7784
www.laderacyclery.com

Laguna Cyclery
240 Thalia Street
Laguna Beach 92651
(949) 494-1522
www.lagunacyclery.net

Orange Cycle
210 South Glassel
Orange 92866
(714) 532-6838
www.orangecycle.com

The Path Bike Shop
215 West First Street
Tustin 92780
(714) 669-0784
www.thepathbikeshop.com

Performance Bike
8850 Warner Avenue
Fountain Valley 92708
(714) 842-3480

Performance Bike
24721 Alicia Parkway
Laguna Hills 92653
(949) 707-0344

Performance Bike
2745 El Camino Real
Tustin 92782
(714) 838-0641

Rainbow Bicycle Company
485 North Coast Highway
Laguna Beach 92651
(949) 497-5806
www.teamrain.com

REI
1411 South Village Way
Santa Ana 92705
(714) 543-4142
www.rei.com

REI
7777 Edinger Avenue
Huntington Beach 92647
(714) 379-1938
www.rei.com

Revo Cycles
34155 Pacific Coast Highway
Dana Point 92629
(949) 496-1995
www.revocycles.com

Richard's Cyclery
11943 Valley View Street
Garden Grove 92845
(714) 379-2717

Rock and Road Cyclery
5701 Santa Ana Canyon Road, Suite F&G
Anaheim Hills 92807
(714) 998-2453
www.rocknroadcyclery.net

Rock and Road Cyclery
27281 La Paz Road
Laguna Niguel 92677
(949) 360-8045
www.rocknroadcyclery.net

Rock and Road Cyclery
6282 Irvine Boulevard
Irvine 92620
(949) 733-2453
www.rocknroadcyclery.net

Rock and Road Cyclery
27825 Santa Margarita Parkway, Suite A
Mission Viejo 92691
(949) 859-5076
www.rocknroadcyclery.net

San Clemente Cyclery
2801 South El Camino Real
San Clemente 92672
(949) 492-8890
www.sccyclery.com

Sand Canyon Cyclery
6616 Irvine Center Drive
Irvine 92618
(949) 450-9906
sandcanyoncyclery.com

Santiago Cycling
115 North Prospect
Tustin 92780
(714) 544-6091
www.cyclingpros.com

Supergo Bike Shop
8850 Warner Avenue
Fountain Valley 92708
(714) 842-3480
www.supergo.com

Surf City Cyclery
7470 Edinger Avenue
Huntington Beach 92647
(714) 842-1717
www.surfcitycyclery.com

Switchback Cyclery
3436 East Chapman Avenue
Orange 92869
(714) 628-3913
www.switchbackcyclery.com

Two Wheeler Dealer Bicycles
1039 East Imperial Highway #f-3
Brea 92821
(714) 671-1730
www.twdcycling.com

Two Wheels One Planet
420 East 17th Street
Costa Mesa 92627
(949) 646-7706
www.twowheelsoneplanet.com

Two Wheels One Planet
24844 Muirlands Boulevard
Lake Forest 92638
(949) 581-8900
www.twowheelsoneplanet.com

APPENDIX C: ORANGE COUNTY MOUNTAIN BIKE GROUPS

Geoladders
An online community that lists mountain bike routes, promotes races, and has a forum to meet other riders and arrange group rides.
www.geoladders.com

Irvine Ranch Land Reserve
Docent-led rides are offered every week on the land reserve.
www.irvineranchlandreserve.org

SHARE
A great advocate for Orange County mountain biking and trail use since 1988. The IMBA-affiliated group hosts weekly rides, maintains trails, and has fun events.
www.sharemtb.com

SoCal Trail Riders
A new group that offers a variety of rides in Orange County and beyond. Sign up on their Web site.
www.socaltrailriders.org

Team Basso
Group rides, mountain bike trips, and trail advocacy. New riders are welcome.
www.teambasso.com

Warrior's Society
A group that rides, advocates for, and maintains trails in the Santa Ana Mountains. They also organize large-scale races in the Santa Anas.
www.warriorssociety.org

INDEX

Index

DEAR CUSTOMERS AND FRIENDS,

SUPPORTING YOUR INTEREST IN OUTDOOR ADVENTURE, travel, and an active lifestyle is central to our operations, from the authors we choose to the locations we detail to the way we design our books. Menasha Ridge Press was incorporated in 1982 by a group of veteran outdoorsmen and professional outfitters. For 25 years now, we've specialized in creating books that benefit the outdoors enthusiast.

Almost immediately, Menasha Ridge Press earned a reputation for revolutionizing outdoors- and travel-guidebook publishing. For such activities as canoeing, kayaking, hiking, backpacking, and mountain biking, we established new standards of quality that transformed the whole genre, resulting in outdoor-recreation guides of great sophistication and solid content. Menasha Ridge continues to be outdoor publishing's greatest innovator.

The folks at Menasha Ridge Press are as at home on a white-water river or mountain trail as they are editing a manuscript. The books we build for you are the best they can be, because we're responding to your needs. Plus, we use and depend on them ourselves.

We look forward to seeing you on the river or the trail. If you'd like to contact us directly, join in at www.trekalong.com or visit us at www.menasharidge.com. We thank you for your interest in our books and the natural world around us all.

SAFE TRAVELS,

BOB SEHLINGER
PUBLISHER